MW01716798

Reading Games and Activities

Mary E. Dorsey

Curriculum Specialist
School Board of Broward County
Fort Lauderdale, Florida

Fearon Publishers, Inc.
Belmont, California

ISBN-0-8224-5810-1

Library of Congress Catalog Card Number: 72-80026

Printed in the United States of America.

PREFACE

The inability of children to read is one of the major areas of concern in today's school program. It is a problem that must be approached with understanding and competence. Many teachers agree that through the use of games, aids, and activities they may help many children who would otherwise fail to reach their potential. *Reading Games and Activities* contains hundreds of original, stimulating ideas for independent and supervised work. These games and activities were developed to assist the teacher in providing detailed individual instruction for each student.

There have been many studies, surveys, investigations, conferences, magazine articles, and books devoted to reading deficiencies. The causes are numerous; and seldom, if ever, can one single factor be isolated as the sole cause. When a pupil is experiencing difficulty in reading, the teacher may conclude that his problems stem from any number of sources—physical, emotional, intellectual, or educational.

What, then, is the role of the classroom teacher? Should she just teach the child to read, or should she spend some time getting to the basic cause of the reading problem? Obviously, a doctor cannot treat a patient before he diagnoses the source of the problem.

Thus, the teacher must assume the role of a diagnostician. She must be extremely capable in the area of diagnosing causes of, and prescribing treatment for, reading deficiencies; and most of all, she must be an expert at evaluating the results of the reading treatment. Even though she may not be qualified to undertake psychotherapy with the child, and although she cannot guarantee the absence of parental rejection or inconsistency, the teacher can accept the child as he is, give him support and security, appreciate and encourage his positive behavior, and in this way create a more wholesome learning atmosphere.

When structuring her reading program, the teacher should keep in mind that no particular procedure should be used too long because the child will become restless and lose interest. Instead, the teacher should provide a variety of short, interesting activities to stimulate the child. This book contains hundreds of such activities, organized by skills—auditory perception of rhyme and of initial consonants; visual-auditory perception of initial and final consonants, long and short vowel sounds, and consonant blends; vocabulary extension and comprehension; and oral language development. There are also chapters on readiness activities and independent activities.

All of the games and activities in this book are an outgrowth of my work as a classroom teacher, a remedial reading teacher, and as a curriculum specialist in the public schools of Broward County, Florida. They have been thoroughly tested and have been found to be successful in improving a child's ability to read. All are adaptable to small groups or to individual use. However, the teacher should feel free to adjust and modify any activity to fit the interests and specific needs of her pupils.

Materials for Constructing Aids

1. Tagboard (manila or white)
2. Posterboard (assorted colors)
3. Showcard board (fourteen-ply)
4. Construction paper
5. "Fadeless" art paper
6. Velour paper
7. Gummed paper
8. Corrugated paper
9. Tracing paper
10. Brown kraft paper
11. Newsprint
12. Art paper
13. Bristol board
14. Felt
15. Masking tape and cellophane tape
16. Paste or cement glue
17. Brass fasteners and staplers
18. Loose-leaf rings
19. Pipe cleaners
20. Scissors
21. Ruler and yardstick
22. Felt-tip markers (regular and thin-line)
23. Needle and thread
24. Colorful pictures
25. Various sizes of cardboard boxes
26. Library card pockets
27. Long white envelopes
28. Cubical blocks
29. Stocking boxes
30. Styrofoam (blocks and sheets)
31. Art gum
32. Sentence strips
33. Manila flashcard strips
34. Paper puncher

Acknowledgment. Grateful acknowledgment is made to Ulysses G. Horne, Director of Migrant Education, Broward County Public Schools, for his moral support and for making it possible for this book to become a reality.

MARY E. DORSEY

CONTENTS

Chapter 1

SEQUENCE OF SKILLS

In reading, as in any other area, there are foundation skills that must be developed before one can move to a more advanced level. The teacher must be extremely familiar with the sequence of skills in order to assure continuity from one level to another. For example, she must know that she should not attempt to teach short vowels before teaching initial consonants unless specified in a particular program.

Any sequence of skills should be flexible enough that a teacher may begin with the skills needed by an individual student. The teacher should not expect each student to begin with the first skill on the list. Thus, if a student's instructional level is third grade, it is unnecessary for the teacher to begin with rhyming. More than likely, the student has mastered the skills up to and including the short vowel sounds. The teacher would begin at the next step on the sequence chart.

The list that follows is a compilation of skills from the most widely used basal reading series.

Word Identification Skills

I. Contextual clues

- Picture clues
- Word-form clues
- Meaning clues
- Word, sentence, and paragraph meaning

II. Phonetic analysis

- Auditory perception of rhymes
- Initial consonant sounds
- Final consonant sounds
- Medial consonant sounds
- Long vowels

Short vowels
Initial and final consonant blends
Three-letter consonant blends
Consonant digraphs
Long and short vowels
Vowels affected by the letter *r*
Vowel digraphs
Vowel dipthongs
Syllabication
Silent letters

III. Structural analysis

Common word ending *s, es, d, ed, ing, er, est*
Words ending in *ed*
  "ed" sound as *ed* in started
  "ed" sound as *ed* in played
  "ed" sound as *ed* in looked
Compound words
Root or base words
Contractions
Possessives
Changes in word forms by:
  Dropping final *e* and adding *ing*
  Doubling the final consonant before adding *ing*
  Changing the *y* to *i* before adding *es*
Soft sound of *c* and *g*
Forming plurals by changing *f* to *v* before adding *es*
Syllabication rules
Accent clues
Prefixes and suffixes

Vocabulary Extension

I. Definition of words or use of dictionary

Accent marks as guides to pronunciation
Alphabetical order
Diacritical marks
Entry words
Appropriate meaning
Pronunciation key
Syllabic division of words

II. Classification

Relationships among words
Categorizing ideas, objects, and opinions
Organization of thought units
Basic understanding of concepts

III. Meanings of words

Service words
Sight vocabulary
Technical terms
Multiple meanings
Contextual clues
Antonyms and synonyms
Homonyms and homophones
Analogies and figurative language

Comprehension

I. Analyze and interpret pictures

Discuss story that picture tells
Name object or characters in picture
Say and write words, phrases, and sentences that may be taken from picture
Write a story from picture
Give the story a title

II. Locating and recalling information

Retain what is read
Read to locate specific details
Sense implied ideas and meanings
Read to obtain main idea of paragraph or story
Reread to find additional facts
Find and read portion that proves or disproves the fact

III. Organizing and reporting information

Follow oral and written directions
Skim and scan to follow a sequence of events and ideas
Summarize facts, ideas, and opinions

IV. Read to evaluate and interpret ideas and opinions

Distinguish fact from opinion
Anticipate or predict expected outcomes

See relationship among details
Consider and judge relevancy of ideas and opinions
Compare the opinions of two or more writers
Draw conclusions and summarize
Form opinions in relationship to what is read

V. **Fundamental study skills**

Securing basic information
Effective use of table of contents
Understanding use of glossary
Knowledge of book parts

VI. **Adequate use of reference materials**

Dictionary skills
Organization and use of encyclopedia
Reading the newspaper
Understanding maps, charts, and other graphical data
Structure of library system
Use of card catalog—alphabetizing of titles, authors, and subjects

VII. **Parts of a book**

Title of book
Understanding the title page
Importance of copyright date
Purpose of preface and acknowledgments
Table of contents
Organization of maps, charts, tables, and illustrations
Chapters
Headings and subheadings
Bibliography, appendix, and index

Master Grouping Continuum

Purpose: To facilitate planning for small group instruction (for the teacher).

Construction: Rule 22″ x 28″ posterboard into ten, twelve, or fifteen squares depending on the number of skills the chart is for. Leave room at the top for the correct heading. In sequential order at the top of each square, print the reading skill to be mastered: Rhyming, Initial Consonants, Consonant Blends, Long Vowels, Short Vowels, etc. Attach library card pockets under each category (*see* illustration).

Utilization: Print the name of each child on a small card and insert the card in the pocket under the particular skill where the student is experiencing difficulty. There may be five students' names inserted under rhyming, four who need help with initial consonants, and several who need additional help with short vowels. At a glance, the teacher is able to get a total picture of the deficiencies of the whole class in skill areas. In addition to the large chart, the teacher should keep a notebook-size copy of the same chart to serve as a detailed lesson plan. Unlike the large chart, this notebook chart should not be changed from week to week. It is kept as a record to show the amount of progress made by each student.

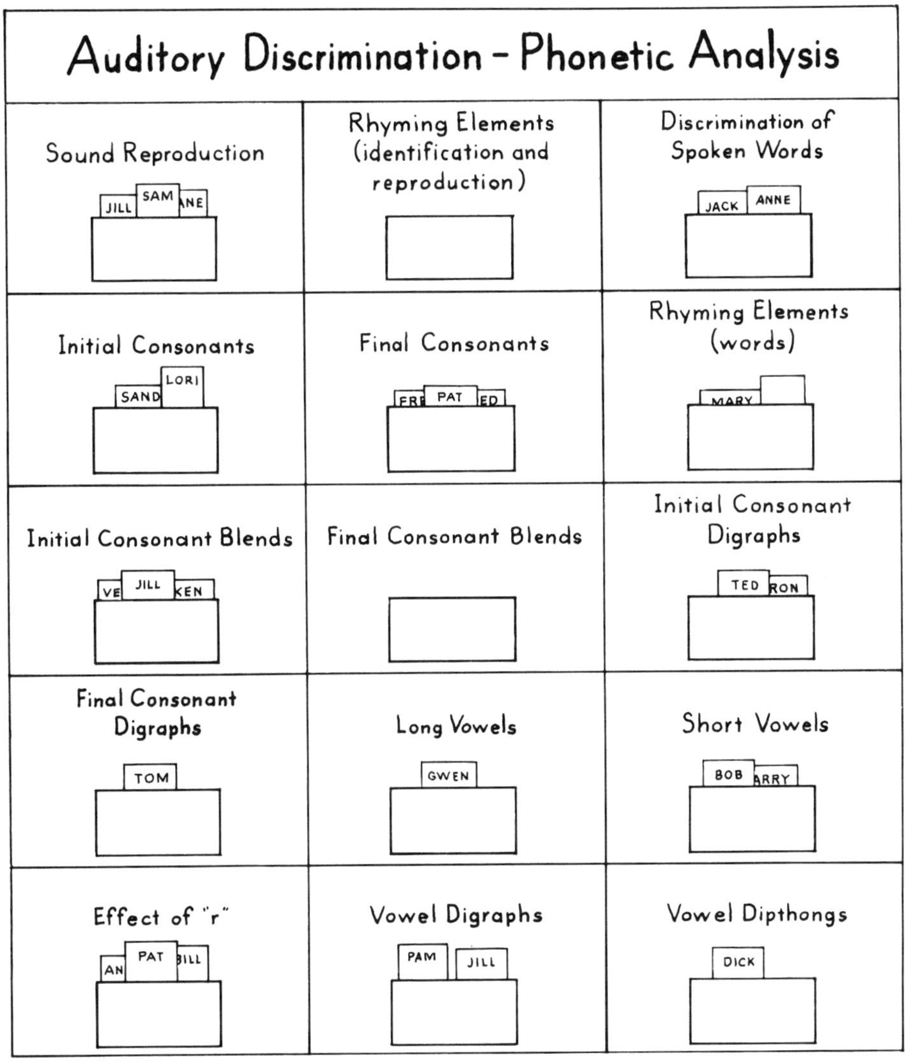

Chapter 2

READINESS ACTIVITIES

Exposing the child to various rich experiences during his early years, such as working and playing cooperatively with others, following simple oral directions, and distinguishing between objects of different sizes, shapes, and colors, will contribute greatly to his reading success in later years.

Research indicates that readiness activities should include some of the following:

1. Exercises and experiences that help to develop an adequate conceptual background.
2. Practice in recognizing likenesses and differences in color, size, and shape.
3. Exercises in the discrimination of letters of the alphabet.

The activities in this chapter are designed to further the child's development during the readiness period.

Alphabet Puzzle

Skill Development: Alphabetical sequence.

Construction: Cut strips of green posterboard 25″ x 4″. Every five inches apart, write a letter of the alphabet in sequential order. Between each letter draw a wide vertical zigzag line. Cut the zigzag line in half so that the line shows on both parts of the puzzle. Make a folder for the puzzle.

Utilization: When the puzzle is put together correctly, the letters will be in alphabetical order. Each puzzle should contain no more than five letters until the child's skill improves.

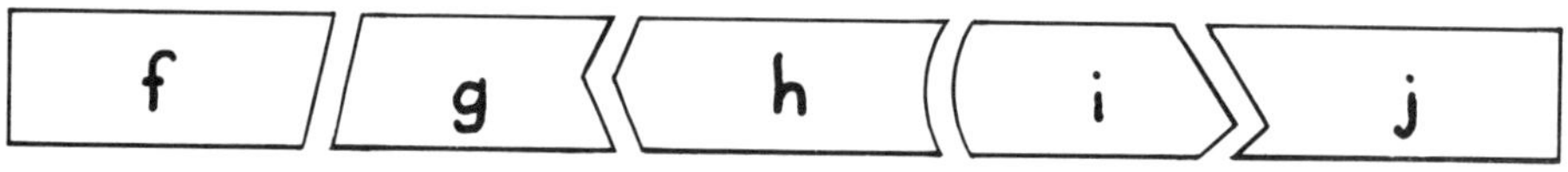

Matching Game

Skill Development: Visual discrimination and visual memory.

Construction: Make one set of large cards to be used by the teacher. Make a set of small cards for each student. Begin with odd designs and move first to capital letters and then to lower case.

Utilization: For visual discrimination exercises, the teacher raises her card and the students hold up a matching card. For visual memory, the teacher raises her card for ten seconds while the students watch. Then the teacher removes her card and asks the students to find the same card and raise it.

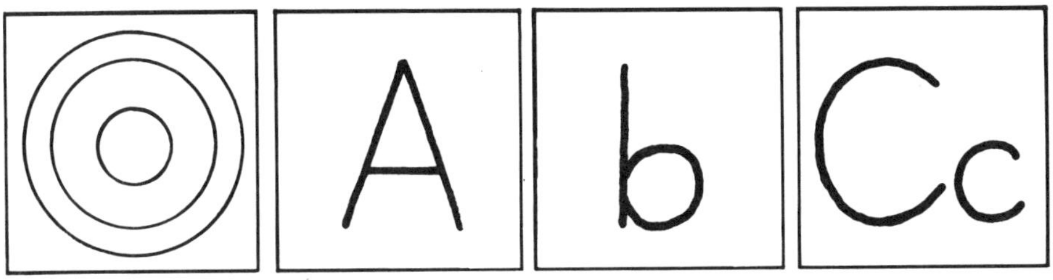

Three-in-a-row

Skill Development: Alphabetical sequence.

Construction: Use tagboard to make a set of twenty-six alphabet cards about the size of regular playing cards. Write a letter on each card and shuffle the cards.

Utilization: Two or three people may play this game. One player deals three cards to each person. The remaining cards are stacked in the center. The object of the game is to get three cards with letters that are in sequential order. In turn, each player takes one card from the top of the stack until he can put down three cards that have sequential letters. Each time a player draws a card from the stack, he must discard one of the cards in his hand. He should never have more than three cards. The player may or may not use the card that he draws from the stack. For example, a player who has *d* and *e* in his hand needs either *c* or *f* to win the game.

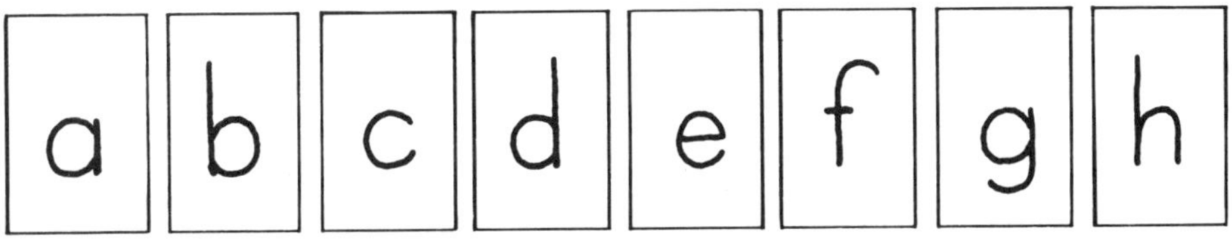

What's Missing?

Skill Development: Alphabetical sequence.

Construction: Draw a chart of spaces on 15″ x 15″ posterboard or tagboard. Write some of the letters in the spaces in alphabetical order and leave other spaces vacant for the students to fill in. Make a set of alphabet cards (3″ x 3″) for the students to use to fill in the vacant spaces. The board may also be covered with a transparent sheet (acetate or ryton) so that pupils can write in the missing letters. Other charts may be constructed to show different letters missing. All charts should have the letters in a left-to-right sequence.

Utilization: The students are to use the letter cards to fill in the missing letters. If the master game board is covered with a transparent cover, the child should use a grease pencil to write in the correct letters.

A		C	D	E	
	H	I	J		
M			P	Q	
S			V		X
	Z				

	b	c		e
f				j
		m		
p		r		t
	v		x	
z				

ABC Accordion Book

Skill Development: Alphabetical sequence, concept building, and color recognition.

Construction: Cut thirteen pieces of heavy 12″ x 14″ colored board. Place two pieces of the board side by side and tape them together with masking tape. Add a third piece, and so on, until all thirteen pieces have been taped together to make an accordion folder that will stand alone. Mount colorful pictures beginning with A through M on the front of the board. Mount pictures N through Z on the back of the board. Put the corresponding letter for each picture in the upper right-hand corner of the board.

Utilization: Ask the pupils to identify the letter, the picture, and the colors used in the picture. Develop meaningful concepts by asking leading questions. For example, with a picture of an igloo, the teacher might ask, "What is an igloo?" "What is it made from?" "Would you find it in Florida?" and so on.

Alphabet Wheel

Skill Development: Alphabetical sequence.

Construction: For each pupil, make a wheel with letters of the alphabet in mixed order. Attach a movable hand to the wheel.

Utilization: When the teacher gives the signal, the pupil turns the hand to a given letter. The pupil must then say the next four letters in sequential order. Example: The hand is on *h*. The student must be able to say *i, j, k, l.*

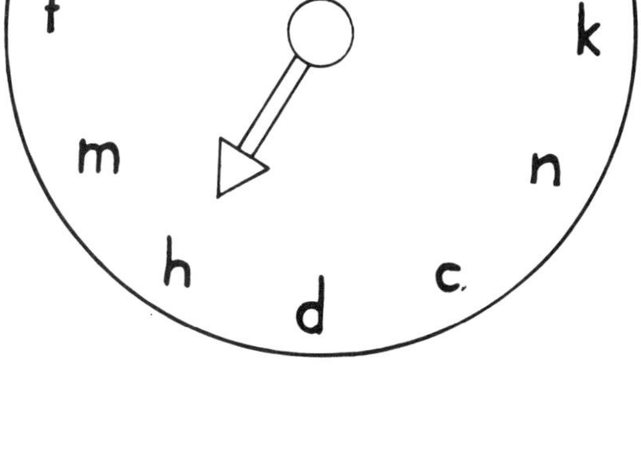

Color Puzzle

Skill Development: Color recognition, eye-hand coordination, and shape recognition.

Construction: Use pink, yellow, green, and blue posterboard. Cut a pink circle 6½″ in diameter, a yellow triangle 8″ x 8″ x 8″, a green square 6″, and a blue rectangle 6″ x 11″. Cut each shape into parts to make a puzzle, and number each part of the puzzle. Cut the circle into two parts, the square into three parts, the triangle into four parts, and the rectangle into five parts. Make a folder for the puzzles when they are not in use.

Utilization: Ask a pupil to take all the pieces of one color from the envelope and put them together to make a shape. Have him identify the color and name the shape that he assembled. The child should begin with the puzzle with the least number of parts and progress to the five-part puzzle.

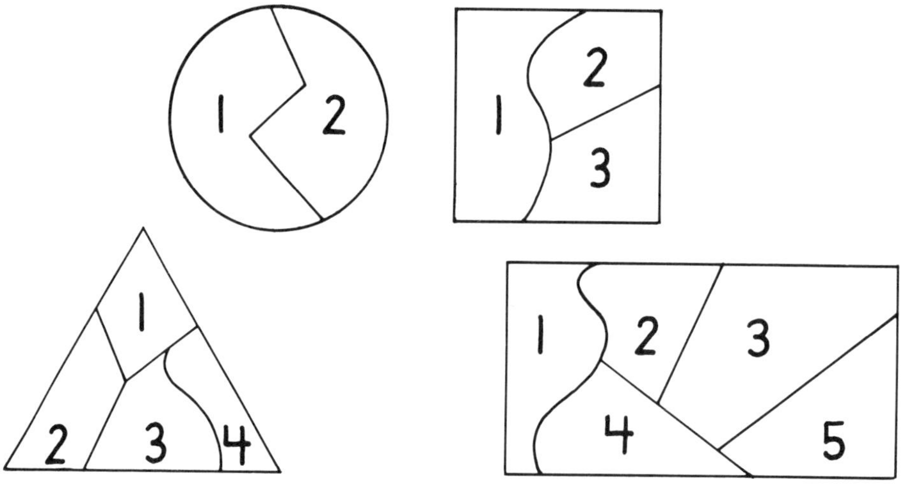

Shape Recognition

Skill Development: Shape recognition and the ability to follow oral directions.

Construction: Cut out a diamond, a circle, a square, a rectangle, an octagon, and a triangle from fourteen-ply showboard. The size of the shapes depends upon what the teacher wishes to put into the pockets. Make a duplicate of each shape and cut the duplicate in half. Staple one half to the lower part of the whole shape to form a pocket at the bottom. Insert pictures, word cards, letter cards, name cards, blend cards, days of the week, months of the year, or any other material.

Utilization: Place these shapes on the bulletin board or wall in reach of the pupils. Ask a student to get the picture of the dog from the square, or from the circle, for example, or to take the name John Brown from the rectangle pocket and put it into the diamond pocket.

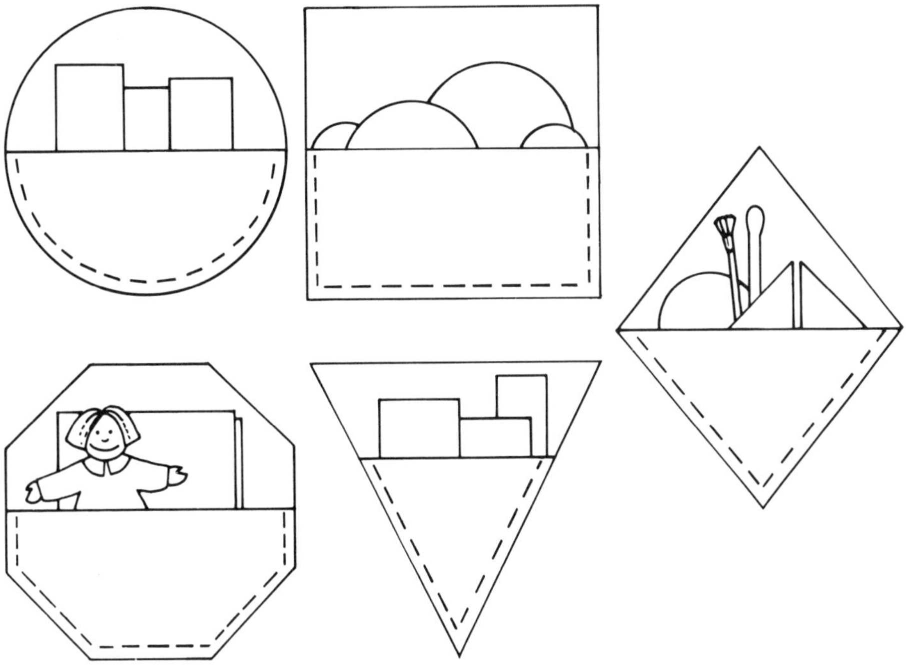

Button Book

Skill Development: Eye-hand coordination, color recognition, number concepts, and classification of clothing.

Construction: Enlarge each of the patterns given here and trace them on durable paper. The patterns are for the following pieces of clothing:

a pair of short *brown* pants—1 button
a pair of long *black* pants with shoulder straps—2 buttons
a *blue* dress—3 buttons
a *pink* skirt—4 buttons
a *green* shirt—5 buttons
a *red* coat—6 buttons
a *white* two-piece suit, skirt and jacket—7 buttons
a long *orange* dress—8 buttons
a *yellow* raincoat—9 buttons
a *gray* vest—10 buttons

Cut buttonholes in the appropriate places on each pattern, Place each pattern on a 9″ x 12″ piece of felt that is the correct color. Using a piece of chalk, mark through the buttonholes onto the background of felt. Sew the buttons on the background where you have made the chalk marks. In this way, the buttons are permanently attached to the felt. The buttons should be various sizes, getting smaller as the number increases. The first button should be the largest and the last buttons should be the smallest. Lay the clothing patterns on the felt backgrounds and use the buttons to attach the patterns to the felt. In a corner of the felt background, print the number corresponding to the amount of buttons. Hold all the pieces of felt together with loose-leaf rings. The book may be taken apart to accommodate more than one child.

Utilization: In order to complete this activity successfully, a child must be able to match the unattached patterns with the correct background by counting the buttons on the background and the buttonholes on the pattern. He should be able to button and unbutton the patterns quickly and identify the names and colors of each piece of clothing.

Shape and Color Wheel

Skill Development: Visual discrimination and shape and color recognition.

Construction: Cut one large wheel eighteen inches in diameter and several smaller wheels twelve inches in diameter. The larger wheel is for the teacher. The smaller wheels are for the students. Draw or paste cutout identical shapes on the large and small wheels. Each shape should be a different color, but all squares should be the same color, all circles should be the same color, and so on.

Utilization: Using their smaller wheels, the pupils imitate what the teacher does. They should identify the shape and color of each figure.

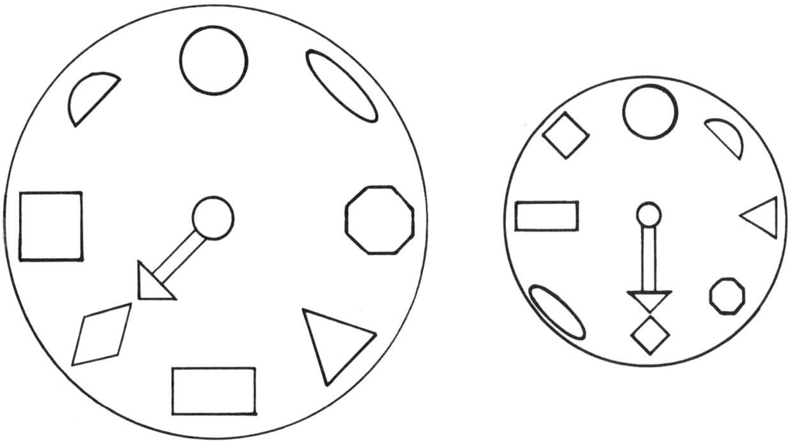

Name Board

Skill Development: Letter recognition, correct name spelling, and left-to-right progression.

Construction: On a 14″ x 11″ piece of showboard, draw enough vertical rules to make blocks for each letter of a student's name. At the top of the board, write in the student's name, one letter to a block. Under the written name, draw horizontal rules to divide the board into four equal rows. Make four letter cards for each letter of the student's name. Staple a piece of board to the back to make a pocket. Insert the letter cards in the pocket on the back of the name card.

Utilization: The student should use the letter cards to spell his name by putting the cards in the correct spaces. Make sure that he begins at the far left and proceeds to the right in a sequential manner.

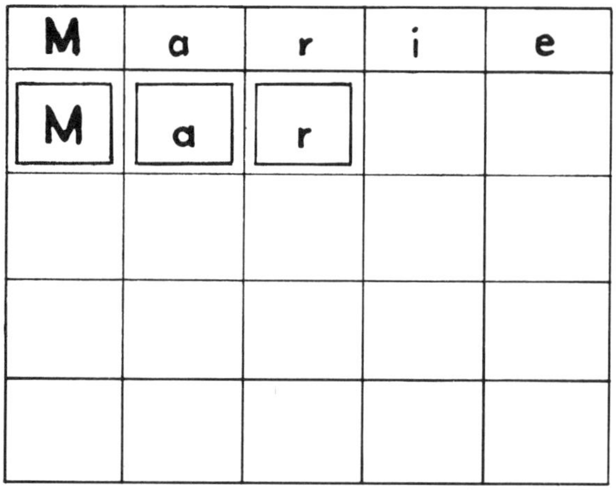

Concept Building Cards

Skill Development: Visual discrimination and meaning concepts.

Construction: Draw two identical sets of fifteen different objects on 9″ x 5″ cards. Some suggestions are shoe, table, house, hammer, ball, flower, boat, umbrella, tree, hat, lamp, truck, book, clock, chair, and fish. You may want to use others that fit your particular teaching lessons.

Utilization: Keep one set of cards and pass the other set out to the students. Raise a card and ask the student who is holding the same card to raise his card. The teacher asks: (a) What is it? (b) What is it used for? (c) Do your mother and father own one? Other questions may be asked to engage the pupil in language development.

Number Clocks

Skill Development: Eye-hand coordination, number recognition, and telling time.

Construction: Cut out one large clock ten inches in diameter to be used by the teacher. Cut out several small clocks six inches in diameter to be used by the students. The clocks can be cut from cardboard. Fasten the hands on with a brad.

Utilization: The teacher turns the hands to four o'clock and asks the students to do the same. If the teacher wishes to give training in visual memory, she may place the hands on her clock, give the students about five seconds to look at her clock, and then turn the clock face down. The students should duplicate the same position on their clocks.

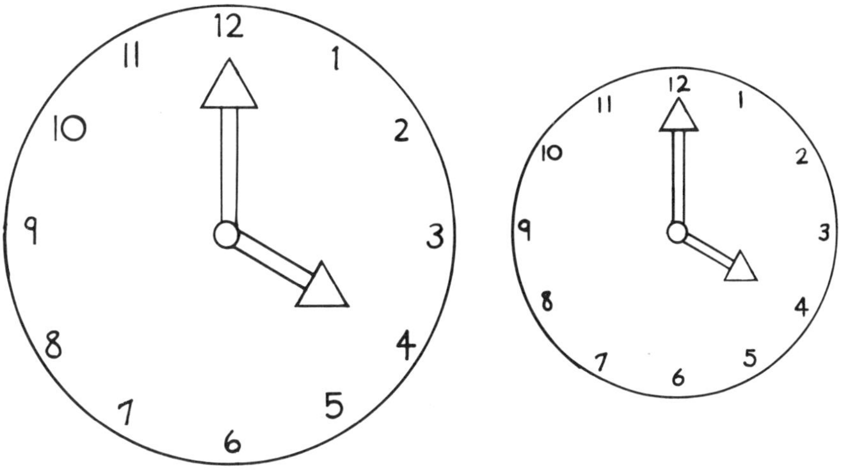

Animals on the Farm

Skill Development: Following written directions, classification, creative expression, number concepts, and positive self-image.

Construction: Enclose 14″ x 9″ newsprint sheets in a wallpaper or felt cover to make a book. Write directions or titles for each page. A sample page is shown here.

Utilization: The student should draw a picture that corresponds to each title or draw as many items as the page states. This activity encourages young readers to work independently.

My Book About Me

Purpose: Teaches student vital information about himself and develops positive self-concept.

Construction: Make a large book (12″ x 18″) by fastening posterboard together with loose-leaf rings. Cover the front page with wallpaper, felt, contact paper, cloth, etc., or let the student draw his favorite picture on the front cover. Insert several pages of paper with one of these titles on each page: About Me, A Picture of Me, A Picture of My Family, My Friends, My School, Me Having Fun. These pages may also be mimeographed and put into booklet form.

Utilization: Have the student fill in each page in his booklet. He should supply the information and draw a picture of his family, his friends, and his school. The student may wish to add other titles to his book, such as: My Wishes, Me at the Park, Food I Like to Eat, etc.

Alphabet Word Box

Skill Development: Initial or final consonants and oral language development.

Construction: Cover stockings boxes or other small boxes with felt or contact paper. Attach a sandpaper or felt letter or a colorful picture to the front of each box.

Utilizations Students are to collect pictures from old magazines and put them in the appropriate boxes. For example, pictures beginning with *p* would go in either of the two boxes shown here. To build concepts and to enhance oral language facilities, the pupils may discuss their pictures in small or large group situations.

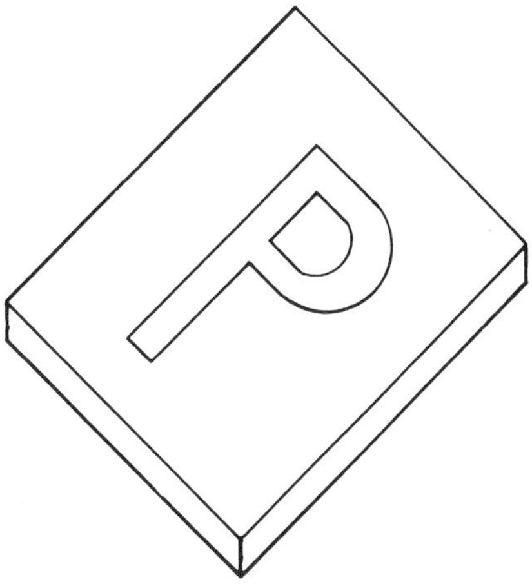

About the Farm

Skill Development: Concept development and vocabulary enrichment and extension.

Construction: Construct a barn using a rectangular cardboard box for the base. Draw a front and rear view of a barn on red corrugated paper. Staple or tape the front view to the front of the box. Tape the rear view to the back. Use black felt to make the door.

Utilization: Use the barn to hold pictures of farm animals, stories about the farms, poems about the farms, and lists of things that are found on farms. If you can find toy tractors, tools, or animals, these may be included also. The students discuss each item in the box and the teacher reads stories about the farm.

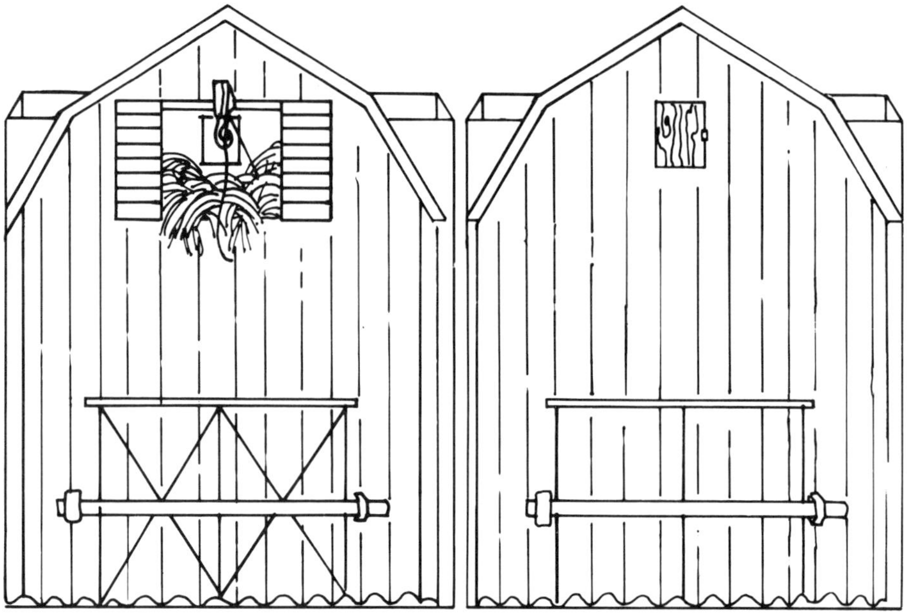

Chapter 3

AUDITORY PERCEPTION OF RHYME

Explain the meaning of rhymes and provide pupils with simple examples (pat-rat), (hill-fill), (can-man), (call-ball). Then start in with the "I Am Thinking" activity. In addition to developing rhyming perception, this activity can be used to diagnose vocabulary meanings or to develop concepts.

I Am Thinking

Part I

1. Say, "I am thinking of a word that rhymes with *bag*. It is red, white, and blue. What is the word?" (flag)
2. I am thinking of a word that rhymes with *came*. It is something that you play. (game)
3. I am thinking of a word that rhymes with *cat*. It is something that you wear on your head. (hat)
4. I am thinking of a word that rhymes with *big*. It goes oink, oink, oink! (pig)
5. I am thinking of a word that rhymes with *hair*. It is something that we sit in. (chair)
6. I am thinking of a word that rhymes with *hook*. It is something to read. (book)
7. I am thinking of a word that rhymes with *best*. It is where a bird lays her eggs. (nest)
8. I am thinking of a word that rhymes with *bed*. It is a color. (red)
9. I am thinking of a word that rhymes with *dish*. It lives in water. (fish)
10. I am thinking of a word that rhymes with *mouse*. We live in it. (house)
11. I am thinking of a word that rhymes with *hill*. We take it when we are sick. (pill)

12. I am thinking of a word that rhymes with *train*. It falls from the sky. (rain)
13. I am thinking of a word that rhymes with *chief*. It is part of a tree. (leaf)
14. I am thinking of a word that rhymes with *owl*. We dry ourselves with it after a bath. (towel)
15. I am thinking of a word that rhymes with *block*. We use it to tell time. (clock)
16. I am thinking of a word that rhymes with *hose*. It is part of the face. (nose)
17. I am thinking of a word that rhymes with *cone*. A dog likes to chew on it. (bone)
18. I am thinking of a word that rhymes with lamp. It is used on a letter. (stamp)
19. I am thinking of a word that rhymes with *cork*. We eat with it. (fork)
20. I am thinking of a word that rhymes with *town*. He is a funny, funny man in a circus. (clown)

Part II

1. I am thinking of a word that rhymes with *stray*. It means to swing from side to side. (sway)
2. I am thinking of a word that rhymes with *reason*. It means the betrayal of one's country. (treason)
3. I am thinking of a word that rhymes with *mold*. It means to speak to someone sharply or rudely. (scold)
4. I am thinking of a word that rhymes with *chest*. It is also called a coat of arms. (crest)
5. I am thinking of a word that rhymes with *space*. It means to make firm and secure by suppying support. (brace)
6. I am thinking of a word that rhymes with *fate*. It means price according to a scale or standard. (rate)
7. I am thinking of a word that rhymes with *stalk*. It's a kind of soft limestone used for writing on a blackboard. (chalk)
8. I am thinking of a word that rhymes with *blame*. It is the glowing part of a fire. (flame)
9. I am thinking of a word that rhymes with *narrow*. It's a small brown bird of the finch family. (sparrow)
10. I am thinking of a word that rhymes with *raft*. It means the selection of men for military service. (draft)
11. I am thinking of a word that rhymes with *thistle*. It is a musical sound made with the lips. (whistle)

12. I am thinking of a word that rhymes with *pocket*. It is a gold or silver case for a photograph worn on a chain around the neck or on a bracelet. (locket)
13. I am thinking of a word that rhymes with *follow*. It means the act of taking a mouthful of food or drink into the stomach. (swallow)
14. I am thinking of a word that rhymes with *brave*. It means a person who must serve another. (slave)
15. I am thinking of a word that rhymes with *sketch*. It means to go and get and bring. (fetch)
16. I am thinking of a word that rhymes with *slang*. It's the long hollow tooth of a poisonous snake. (fang)
17. I am thinking of a word that rhymes with *single*. It is a thin, flat piece of wood or other material used to cover roofs. (shingle)
18. I am thinking of a word that rhymes with *nimble*. It's a metal cover to protect the end of a finger in sewing. (thimble)
19. I am thinking of a word that rhymes with *faint*. It means pleasingly old-fashioned in looks or ways. (quaint)
20. I am thinking of a word that rhymes with *puzzle*. It's a device used to cover a dog's mouth to keep him from biting. (muzzle)
21. I am thinking of a word that rhymes with *weather*. It is the tanned skin or hide of an animal. (leather)
22. I am thinking of a word that rhymes with *wedge*. It means near the brink or border. (edge)
23. I am thinking of a word that rhymes with *dwell*. It means to calm or put down as in a riot or rebellion. (quell)
24. I am thinking of a word that rhymes with *slink*. It means to cause to get smaller by wetting and drying. (shrink)
25. I am thinking of a word that rhymes with *rage*. This is the raised flooring in an auditorium. (stage)
26. I am thinking of a word that rhymes with *shallow*. It's the melted fat of cattle and sheep used in making candles. (tallow)
27. I am thinking of a word that rhymes with *engaged*. It means to become very angry or irritated. (enraged)
28. I am thinking of a word that rhymes with *certain*. It's a hanging screen or cloth that can be drawn up and let down or fastened to one side. (curtain)
29. I am thinking of a word that rhymes with *delay*. It means to rot or waste away or change from a sound to an unsound state. (decay)
30. I am thinking of a word that rhymes with *deprive*. It means to recover consciousness and strength, as a person after sickness or injury. (revive)

Pictures That Rhyme

Hold up a picture. The pupil must choose from several pictures in his hand and hold up the rhyming picture. For example, if the teacher held up a picture of a log, the child would select the picture of a dog.

Which Word Is Different?

1. Say, "Listen as I say some words: *dog, log, sit, frog.* Which word is different?" The child would answer *sit.*
2. Beat, boot, seat, meat, heat. Which word is different? (boot)
3. Line, spend, sign, fine, mine. Which word is different? (spend)
4. Bit, sit, wit, hit, tell. (tell)
5. Sing, ring, dish, king, swing. (dish)
6. Stole, stall, shawl, ball, call. (stole)
7. House, louse, mouse, spouse, rice. (rice)
8. Prank, rank, rap, thank, drank. (rap)
9. Slab, slip, scab, crab, grab. (slip)
10. Doll, dell, swell, smell, spell. (doll)
11. Trot, spot, scat, blot, knot. (scat)
12. Sped, sled, led, wed, pod. (pod)
13. Drill, bell, chill, dill, spill. (bell)
14. Jump, bump, lump, step, clump. (step)
15. Feet, sleep, sheep, steep, weep. (feet)
16. Stream, team, cream, seam, pen. (pen)
17. Than, thin, chin, spin, fin. (than)
18. Back, snake, shake, lake, stake. (back)
19. Drip, trip, slip, pep, flip. (pep)
20. Chick, stick, peck, slick, tick. (peck)

Rhyming Completions

Part I

1. Say, "The little old lady ran out of the *house* because she saw a tiny ________." Ask the pupils to complete the sentence. The completion word should be a rhyming word. (mouse)
2. As we rode home on the *train,* the sky grew dark and it began to ________. (rain)
3. The day was clear, the weather was *cool,* as we took our books and started for________. (school)
4. We ran and jumped with *glee* and then we climbed a________. (tree)

5. When the circus came to *town,* we went to see the funny________. (clown)
6. What do you *think.* I have a beautiful dress that is a lovely shade of ________. (pink)
7. Our teacher read a funny *fable* as we sat around the________. (table)
8. For dinner we ate salad and *steak,* and for dessert we ate some ________. (cake)
9. The men dug a very large *hole* in order to find the black, hard ________. (coal)
10. The doctor said, "If you're very *smart,* you will take good care of your ________." (heart)
11. "I am very, very wooly, yes, I *am*" said the little baby________. (lamb)
12. They could hear the loud *sound* when they put their ears to the ________. (ground)
13. He was very old and had one *leg,* but he was proud and would not ________. (beg)
14. I went to the store and then to the *bank,* and on the way home I saw Uncle________. (Frank)
15. I was on my way to open the *door* when I slipped and fell on the ________. (floor)
16. As I sat down to eat, my mother *said,* "You may have some jelly and ________." (bread)
17. I went out the door and stood on the *grass* just as the parade was about to________. (pass)
18. The birds did sing, the birds did *fly,* high up into the________. (sky)
19. The little old lady nodded her *head,* put down her book, and went to________. (bed)
20. The little old frog jumped about in the *pool.* It was a very hot day and he wanted to keep________. (cool)
21. Many little children live on my *street.* There's always the sound of little________. (feet)
22. It's very nice to go for a *ride.* Just open the car door and jump ________. (inside)
23. When I lie down to rest, soft music is what I like________. (best)
24. We climbed up on the merry-go-*round.* The music has such a lively ________. (sound)

Part II

1. The diver aimed and hit his *mark.* He had killed a man-eating ________. (shark)

2. My father is a preacher. But I think I'll be a________. (teacher)
3. It is too far away to *hike.* So I think I will ride my________. (bike)
4. My friend Alice wanted to be *cool.* So she decided to jump into the swimming________. (pool)
5. Which do you like the *most?* Pancakes, waffles, or French________? (toast)
6. As we walked along the *shore,* we saw a small grocery________. (store)
7. She had on a beautiful *dress.* But she dropped her candy and what a ________! (mess)
8. Our band will march down the *street.* Don't forget to watch our ________. (feet)
9. I wanted some cake, just one *slice.* But I could not afford to pay the ________. (price)
10. Sometimes the smell of fresh *paint* can cause a person to________. (faint)
11. When you stand near the *fountain,* you can see the top of the ________. (mountain)
12. Have you seen the beautiful *queen?* She's the cutest girl I've ever ________. (seen)
13. I think I'll get some fresh *air.* Would you please bring me a________? (chair)
14. We decided it was too *cool* to go swimming in the________. (pool)
15. He found his favorite *toy.* He clapped his hands and jumped for ________. (joy)
16. The young lady lost her *poise* when she heard the loud________. (noise)
17. Be sure to wrap the meat in aluminum *foil* so that it will not________. (spoil)

Rhyming Verses

Part I

1. The teacher says, "Jack be nimble. Jack be quick. Jack jump over the candlestick. What are the two words that rhyme?" (quick, stick)
2. Hickory, dickory, dock.
   The mouse ran up the clock.
   (hickory, dickory) (dock, clock)
3. Hey, diddle, diddle.
   The cat and the fiddle.
   (diddle, fiddle)

4. Humpty Dumpty sat on a wall.
Humpty Dumpty had a great fall.
(wall, fall)
5. Sing a song of sixpence,
A pocket full of rye.
Four-and-twenty blackbirds,
Baked in a pie.
(rye, pie)
6. Mary had a little lamb.
It's fleece was white as snow.
And everywhere that Mary went,
The lamb was sure to go.
(snow, go)
7. Pease porridge hot,
Pease porridge cold,
Pease porridge in the pot,
Nine days old.
(hot, pot) (cold, old)
8. There was a crooked man,
And he walked a crooked mile,
He found a crooked sixpence,
Against a crooked stile.
(mile, stile)
9. Baa, Baa black sheep,
Have you any wool?
Yes sir, yes sir,
Three bags full.
(wool, full)
10. A farmer went riding upon his gray mare,
Bumpety, bumpety, bump!
With his daughter behind him so rosy and fair,
Lumpety, lumpety, lump!
(mare, fair) (bump, lump)
11. When supper time is almost come,
But not quite here,
I cannot wait,
And so I take my china mug,
And go down by the milking gate.
(wait, gate)
12. I have a little shadow that goes in and out with me,
And what can be the use of him is more than I can see.
He is very, very like me from his heels up to his head,

And I see him jump before me when I jump into my bed.
(me, see) (head, bed)

13. Brown bunny sits inside his burrow,
Till everything is still.
Then out he slips along the furrow,
Or up the grassy hill.
(burrow, furrow) (still, hill)

14. Oh, isn't it fun when the rain comes down?
I like to go walking way down in the town.
The wind blows in gusts with all of its might.
And makes my umbrella dance—just like a kite.
(down, town) (might, kite)

15. A cock saw the sun as he climbed up the east;
Good morning sir sun, it's high time you appear;
I've been calling you up for an hour at least;
I'm ashamed of your slowness at this time of year.
(east, least) (appear, year)

16. To stretch asleep on the deck in the sun
Or to doze in a sail that's furled;
And at night to make the gray rats run
That's the way to see the world!
(sun, fun) (furled, world)

17. Dreams are made in the moon my dear,
On her shiny hillsides steep!
Pleasant and dreadful and gay and queer
They're piled in a silver heap.
(dear, queer) (steep, heap)

18. A flying squirrel is the strangest thing!
He hasn't a feather. He hasn't a wing.
Yet through the air he skims and scoots.
He doesn't fly. He parachutes.
(thing, wing) (scoots, parachutes)

19. The night was coming very fast;
It reached the gate as I ran past.
The pigeons had gone to the tower of the church,
And all the hens were on their perch.
(fast, past) (church, perch)

20. "There's a tune," said a sly Bengalese,
"Which will charm any snake that you please!
Take a long heavy stick;
Hit the snake with it—quick!
Then proceed with the tune at your ease."
(Bengalese, please, ease) (stick, quick)

Part II

1. Make new friends but keep the old,
   Those are silver, these are gold. (old, gold)
2. I think that I shall never see
   A poem as lovely as a tree. (see, tree)
3. Once upon a summer's day
   A lost dog found its way. (day, way)
4. I never saw a night so black
   That one could not see a track. (black, track)
5. May I live from day to day
   In such a friendly way. (day, way)
6. A swan is so snowy white
   Sailing in the new dawn light. (white, light)
7. A little light is going by
   Going up to see the sky. (by, sky)
8. Bananas are long and yellow
   Plump and ripe and very mellow. (yellow, mellow)
9. When my mother sweeps the room
   She dances with the broom. (room, broom)
10. Where am I going? I don't quite know
    Down to the stream where the flowers grow. (know, grow)

Quiz Panel

Select a panel of four pupils for each team. Begin the game by pronouncing a word for Team A, Player 1. Player 1 gives a rhyming word for five points. The teacher then pronounces a word for Team B, Player 1, and he gives a rhyming word for five points. The teacher or caller proceeds to each team member alternately until every member answers. If one team cannot give a rhyming word, the other team may answer. In case of a tie, have bonus words for the first hand raised.

Using this list of suggested words, the teacher calls the first word. The remaining words are possible responses.

1. farm, charm, harm, alarm
2. feet, sweet, beet, cheat, fleet
3. bone, cone, phone, moan, alone
4. tire, fire, sire, hire
5. sunny, bunny, funny, money
6. corn, horn, torn, born
7. feast, least, beast, east
8. wife, knife, life, strife
9. cattle, rattle, tattle, battle

10. pocket, locket, socket
11. sorrow, borrow, tomorrow
12. merry, berry, ferry
13. score, shore, more, galore
14. matter, chatter, platter, clatter
15. sink, pink, link, mink, wink
16. whistle, bristle, thistle
17. new, view, threw
18. wrinkle, tinkle, twinkle, sprinkle
19. listen, glisten, christen
20. list, wrist, fist, twist
21. bare, care, share, scare
22. lunch, crunch, munch, bunch
23. bright, light, slight, tight
24. mother, other, brother
25. crank, thank, sank, bank
26. year, tear, dear, near
27. taught, aught, brought, caught
28. ghost, host, toast, roast, most
29. fret, get, set, met, net, pet, bet
30. leather, feather, weather, tether
31. carry, marry, scary, tarry
32. finger, linger, swinger, ringer
33. rabbit, habit, limit
34. loud, proud, cloud, crowd, meowed
35. seven, heaven, leaven, eleven
36. treasure, measure, pleasure
37. ever, never, sever, lever
38. teacher, preacher, creature, feature
39. navy, gravy, wavy
40. nation, station, ration, reservation

Yes or No

Instruct each student to make a *yes* and a *no* card. The teacher calls a group of words. If all the words rhyme, the student should hold up the *yes* card. If all of the words don't rhyme, the student should show the *no* card.

1. flop, lot, cot, rot, pot
2. sock, rock, dock, mop, clock
3. cob, pop, rob, sob, mob
4. net, wet, pet, set, pit

5. wag, wig, fig, dig, big
6. rack, black, stack, slack
7. well, tell, till, fell, bell
8. dust, must, rust, risk, gust
9. win, won, tin, pin, spin
10. champ, lamp, stamp, ramp
11. west, duck, nest, pest, best
12. hole, role, sole, pole
13. feet, street, sweet, meet, feel
14. sheep, steep, peep, weep
15. tray, train, clay, gray, play
16. seal, mail, rail, sail, bail
17. meal, beat, meat, eat, seat
18. coat, goat, boat, goal, vote
19. drain, chain, brain, gain, steep
20. broom, droop, bloom, room, zoom
21. nook, book, sharp, shook, brook
22. yellow, fellow, mellow, bellow
23. fish, wish, dish, swish

Rhyming Box

Skill Development: Auditory perception of rhyming elements.

Construction: Cover a twelve-inch-square box with contact paper or cloth. On the outside, attach rhyming pictures. Put several items that have rhyming elements into the box.

Utilization: The child reaches in, selects one item, and identifies it. He gives as many words as he can that rhyme with that item. He gets two points for each rhyming word that he gives. For example, if a child took a ball from the box, correct responses would include hall, fall, stall, call, etc. The idea is to see who gets the highest score.

Items for Box	*Responses*
book	cook, look, hook, brook, shook
stick	click, lick, kick, pick, sick, tick, thick
block	lock, rock, sock, clock, dock, knock
nail	pail, fail, tail, sail, rail, trail
bell	shell, sell, well, tell, fell, smell
drum	gum, hum, dumb, bum, numb, mum
car	far, bar, tar, star, are, jar
train	rain, gain, plane, vain, pain
hat	bat, cat, rat, that, fat, sat

rice	nice, ice, mice, slice, price
spoon	moon, soon, noon, tune
match	catch, patch, latch, batch
ball	hall, call, fall, all, wall
cap	map, lap, tap, nap, trap, wrap
boat	coat, goat, wrote, note
wheel	feel, peel, reel, heel, meal
tack	rack, sack, back, black, pack
glass	pass, class, grass, gas, brass
stamp	lamp, camp, damp, clamp

Chapter 4

AUDITORY PERCEPTION OF INITIAL CONSONANTS

The ultimate goal of auditory training with initial sounds is to alert the child to the different sounds of words, words with the same beginnings, and words with different beginnings. It is imperative that the child be able to distinguish these differences and similarities in order to prepare him for the word recognition process that follows.

Short Stories

1. The teacher says, "*Bill* has a *baseball*. He likes to play *ball* with his good friends, *Bob* and *Barry*. Can you think of a word that begins like *ball*?"
2. Our *family* went on a picnic *Friday*. *Fred* went with us. His mother and *father* went, too. Can you think of a word that begins like *father*?
3. *Today* is *Tuesday*. We will *take* a *trip to town*. Our *teacher* will *take* us. Can you think of a word that begins like *teacher*?
4. The *monkey* is a funny animal with a long tail. He likes to jump from place to place. Can you think of another word that begins like *monkey*?
5. *Have* you *heard* about the three little pigs? One lived in a brick *house*. Another lived in a straw *house*, and the third lived in a *house* made of sticks. Can you think of other words that begin like *house*?
6. *Jack* and *John* went to visit their grandparents in an airplane. It made a loud noise when it took off. It was a *jet* plane. What are some other words that begin like *jet*?
7. *Katherine* has a funny *kitten*. He likes to sleep in the *kitchen*. *Can* you name other words that begin like *kitchen*? (*Note:* Words with the *k* sound as in *cat* are also acceptable.)
8. *Patty* has a fat *pig* for a *pet*. She keeps her *pig* in a *pen*. Name some other words that begin like *pig*.

9. *Gary* got a toy *gun* for a *gift.* He had fun shooting his *gun.* What are some other words that begin like *gun*?
10. *Robert* likes to go hunting with his father. They do not hunt for deer or birds, but they hunt for *rabbits.* Can you think of other words that begin like *rabbit*?
11. "*Linda,*" said the teacher, "Come to the front of the room and stand on your *left leg.*" Can you think of other words that begin like *leg*?
12. *Nell* sleeps every day until *noon. Nell's* dog wants to play ball. But *Nell naps* on and on. What are some other words that begin like *nap*?
13. Fred will begin school on *Thursday. There* will be *thirty* other boys and girls in his class in *third* grade. Can you *think* of other words that begin like *third*?
14. *Charles* is a new boy at school. The *children* are very nice to him. They let him *choose* his favorite *chair. Charles* came from *China.* What are some other words that begin like *China*?
15. *Sandra* went to the beach *Sunday. Sally* and *Susan* went too. They had fun building houses in the *sand.* Name some other words that begin like *sand.*
16. Alan went to the park *yesterday.* He wore his *yellow* jacket. Everyone was there, the old and *young.* Name some other words that begin like *young.*
17. *Dan* and *Don* are twins. They have a *dog* named *Daisy. Daisy* likes to *dig deep* holes in the sand. What are some other words that begin like *dog*?
18. *Willie* stood at the *window watching* the *wind* blow. He saw *women walking* to *work.* He knew that it *would* soon be *winter.* Can you think of other *words* that begin like *winter*?
19. The *shoemaker* is *short* and fat. His *shop* is near the *shore.* He mends *shoes* every day. He likes to *shine* them too. Can you think of other words that begin like *shoe*?
20. *Virginia* went to *visit* her aunt who lived in a small *village.* She had a *very* nice *vacation.* Can you think of other words that begin like *vacation*?
21. The children like to visit the *zoo.* They enjoy looking at the animal with many stripes. He is called a *zebra.* Can you think of other words that begin like *zebra*?

Packing My Bag

The teacher says the first sentence. The children are to finish the second sentence by naming things that they would take with them. The first letter of each item must begin with the same sound as the place they are visiting.

1. The teacher might say, "I'm going to the *beach*." The student says, "I will take a boat, a ball, a bat, a bucket, a balloon, a book, and a beef sandwich."
2. I am going to the *fair*. I will take my family, my friend, some firecrackers, a football, and some food.
3. I am going on a *trip*. I will take a toy, a towel, a toothbrush, some toothpaste, my travel bag, and a turkey sandwich.
4. I am going to *Massachusetts*. I will take some money, a machine, some medicine, a pair of moccasins, some marbles, and my mother.
5. I am going *hunting*. I will take a horse, a harpoon, a hatchet, a hammer, a hoe, and a hamburger.
6. I am going on a *journey*. I will take a jacket, a jeep, some juice, and a jam sandwich.
7. I am going to *Kentucky*. I will take my kite, my kitten, a key, and some ketchup.
8. I am going to *Poland*. I will take some paper, a pencil, a picture, a pipe, a penny, and my papa.
9. I am going to the *garden*. I will take some gum, a gun, a goat, a girl, and a gift.
10. I am going to *Rochester*. I will take a radio, a ring, a raincoat, a robe, a rug, and some ribbon.
11. I am going to *Lansing*. I will take luggage, a letter, a leaf, and a lantern.
12. I am going to *North* Carolina. I will take a note, a nickel, a newspaper, a nurse, and a neighbor.
13. I am going to *Salem*. I will take a sack, some soap, a sandwich, soup, and a sailor.
14. I am going to *Detroit*. I will take a dollar, a dish, a doll, a dog, a doctor, and a dentist.
15. I am going to *Washington*. I will take a wagon, a watch, a waiter, a wife, and a wallet.
16. I am going to *Boston*. I will take a bag, a bicycle, a bugle, a bundle, and a book.
17. I am going to *Dallas*. I will take a dime, a dollar, a dog, a doll, and a dinner.
18. I am going to *town*. I'm going to buy a tire, a table, a tub, and a television.
19. I went to visit the *farm*. I saw a fox, a fish, a fire, and some furniture.
20. I went to the *house*. I got a hat, a horn, and a hammer.
21. I am going to *Japan*. I will see a jet, jewels, junk, jelly, and a judge.
22. She came from *Paris*. She brought a picture, a package, a parrot, and a passport.
23. I was in the *garden*. I saw a goat, a gate, a goose, and a girl.

24. I went for a *ride*. I saw a raincoat, a reindeer, a river, and a rabbit.
25. I went for a *walk*. I saw a window, a well, a wagon, a waiter, and a wolf.
26. I am going *shopping*. I will buy a shirt, shoes, a shawl, shampoo, and shrimp.
27. I went to *Chile*. I saw a chair, a church, a chicken, and a chain.
28. Let's go on a *picnic*. We will take paper, pencil, pepper, pickles, and my pet.
29. I went on *vacation*. I saw a valley, some vegetables, a village, and a violin.
30. I am going into the back *yard*. I will take some yarn, my yo-yo, a yardstick, my yearbook, a yellow chair, and another youngster.

Surprise Box

Put small objects such as toys, buttons, a ruler, a pencil, a marble, a key, etc., in a box. The child reaches in and pulls out an object. He names the object and then he gives another word that begins with the same sound. He gets two points for each correct word. The child with the highest score is the winner.

Four Words

Say, "Listen as I say a group of words. All of the words except one begin with the same sound. *Beat, sand, bun.* Which word began with a different sound?" (sand) "The other words begin with what sound?" (b)

1. bell, ball, bat, cow (cow)
2. belt, camp, bag, bunny (camp)
3. gun, barn, bird, bacon (gun)
4. me, man, my, day (day)
5. hat, mail, money, monkey (hat)
6. meat, dad, moon, map (dad)
7. table, nut, tail, top (nut)
8. hoe, hay, hand, meat (meat)
9. hat, beg, head, horse (beg)
10. party, nail, pan, pie (nail)
11. nut, nine, nest, barn (barn)
12. day, door, hand, dish (hand)
13. corn, walk, water, wish (corn)
14. girl, gun, flag, gas (flag)
15. cake, jam, comb, cookies (jam)
16. June, nose, July, joke (nose)

Tongue Twisters

Say a sentence in which the same sound occurs more than once in the initial or final position. "Betty baked a big batch of butterscotch brownies." Ask the pupil to identify the sound that is heard most. Let the children make up their own.

1. Polly Payton peeled a pink peach for her pet parrot.
2. David and Dan decided to dig a deep, dark ditch.
3. Tillie the turtle took a terrible tumble from the table.
4. The gay goose gave a gift of golden eggs.
5. Sam the sailor sat on a sack singing a sad song.
6. Mary Marshall made merry music on Monday morning.
7. The fat fox followed Fanny around the foggy farm.
8. The red rooster ran down the road after the rabbit.
9. Nick and Nancy never make noise near their nervous neighbor.
10. Happy Harry has a hundred holes in his hat.
11. Bad Billy bit the beautiful baby on the bottom of his foot.
12. Cathy Carter sat in the car calling her cousin Cora.
13. Jimmy Jones jumped in the jerky jeep and drove to the junkyard.
14. Larry Landers took a long look at the little lame lamb.
15. Valerie lived in a very large vacation village in the valley.
16. Willie Watson went walking Wednesday in the winter weather to watch the wonderful woodlands.
17. Pretty Patty put a pound of pears in the pail.
18. Peter Powell put a pack of peanuts in his pants pocket.
19. Dolly Dimple dashed in the door and danced with Danny Davis.
20. Billy Battle bought a box of balls and bats.
21. Silly Sally saw the sun setting in the summer.
22. Fat Fanny fooled a fox at the fair.
23. Get a gallon of good goulash from the galley.
24. Henry Holland hardly had a hundred hats.
25. Lift your left leg and take a long leap over the lamp.
26. A mad monkey munched his meal on the mat.
27. Nancy the nurse never knew the name of her niece.
28. Send Suzy to see Santa on Sunday.
29. Wacky Willy went to the window to watch the wagon.
30. Forty fishermen found a fountain filled with fish.

Matching Pictures

Each child is given a set of pictures representing words that begin with initial consonants. Cut the pictures from old magazines and mount them on tagboard. The teacher has larger pictures beginning with the same sounds. When the teacher raises her picture, she calls on a pupil to raise his picture with the corresponding initial sound.

Department Store

One pupil begins the game by saying, "I went to the department store and I bought a *belt*." Another pupil says, "I went to the department store and I bought a *belt* and a *book*." The next pupil must repeat the *belt* and *book* before he adds another word that begins with the same sound.

Chapter 5

VISUAL-AUDITORY PERCEPTION OF INITIAL AND FINAL CONSONANTS

These games and activities initiate the word attack process that was referred to in Chapter 4. After the child has had several exercises to practice his competency in discriminating between like and unlike sounds, he should be ready to be exposed to the written word along with the sounds.

Tachistoscopic Devices

Skill Development: Word recognition.

Construction: Draw a picture of an object to serve as a clue for the group of words. (For example, draw a church for *ch* words or a ball for words beginning with *b*.) Cut out the picture and cut two slots in it. Write the words on a three-inch-wide strip of tagboard. Insert the strip through the slots. The words should be exposed one at a time when the strip is pulled.

Utilization: The child reads each word as it appears in the "window."

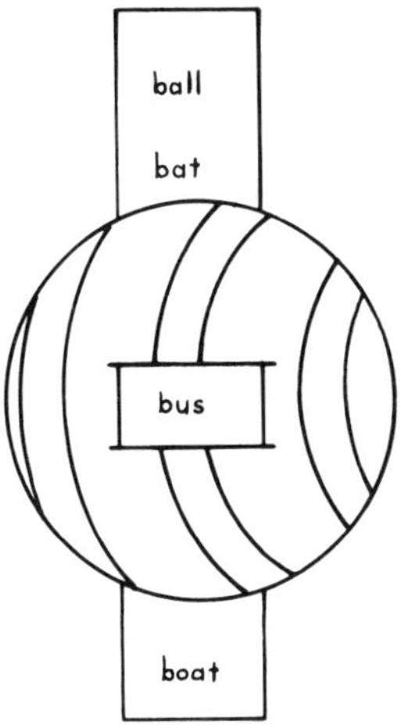

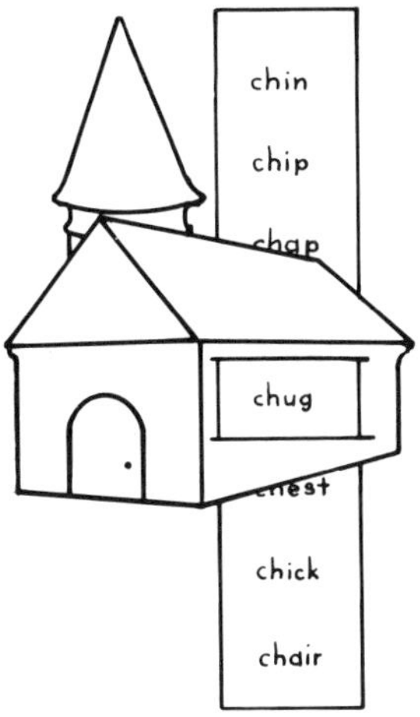

Consonant Bingo

Skill Development: Letter recognition and visual and auditory perception of initial or final sounds.

Construction: Cut several pieces of posterboard 15″ x 15″. Draw nine five-inch squares, three across and three down. Write a consonant in each square, using lowercase and uppercase letters. Attach a library card pocket to the back of each card to hold small pictures of things whose names begin or end with the consonants that appear on the card.

Utilization: *First application.* Give each pupil a card. The consonants should not be in the same order on any two cards. The teacher or a pupil calls a word. The student should cover the beginning or ending consonant of the word. If the word *flag* is called, the consonant *f* or *g* would be covered on the card. Bottle caps or beans may be used as covers. The first person who gets a straight row down, across, or diagonally wins the game. The list of words may be taken from current reading material. *Second application.* The student removes the corresponding picture from the pocket on the back of the card. He then matches the pictures with the correct consonant sounds. For example, the student would cover the letter *g* with a picture of a flag or a picture of a glass. The first student who completely covers his card wins the game. The student who wins is asked to give the beginning or ending sound of each picture on his card. (Pictures may be cut from old workbooks and magazines or purchased from local supply companies.)

Mm	Tt	Pp
Nn	Dd	Gg
Ll	Rr	Ss

Pictures

man–gum
turtle–suit
pot–soap
nest–spoon
door–bread
gun–bug
leaf–pencil
rug–chair
sandwich–dress

House of Consonants

Skill Development: Visual and auditory perception of initial consonants.

Construction: Draw an outline of a simple house. It should be about twenty inches wide and twenty-eight inches tall. Draw a door and a chimney and attach ten library card pockets to hold pictures. Attach a larger felt pocket on the back to hold all the pictures. Write the consonants on the card pockets or write them on tagboard and paper clip them to the pocket for easy changing.

Utilization: Two or three students may use this activity at the same time. Ask the students to remove all pictures from the back pocket and put them in a stack face down. Each student pulls a card and then inserts it in the correct pocket. For example, the picture of the *nurse* would go in the pocket marked *n*.

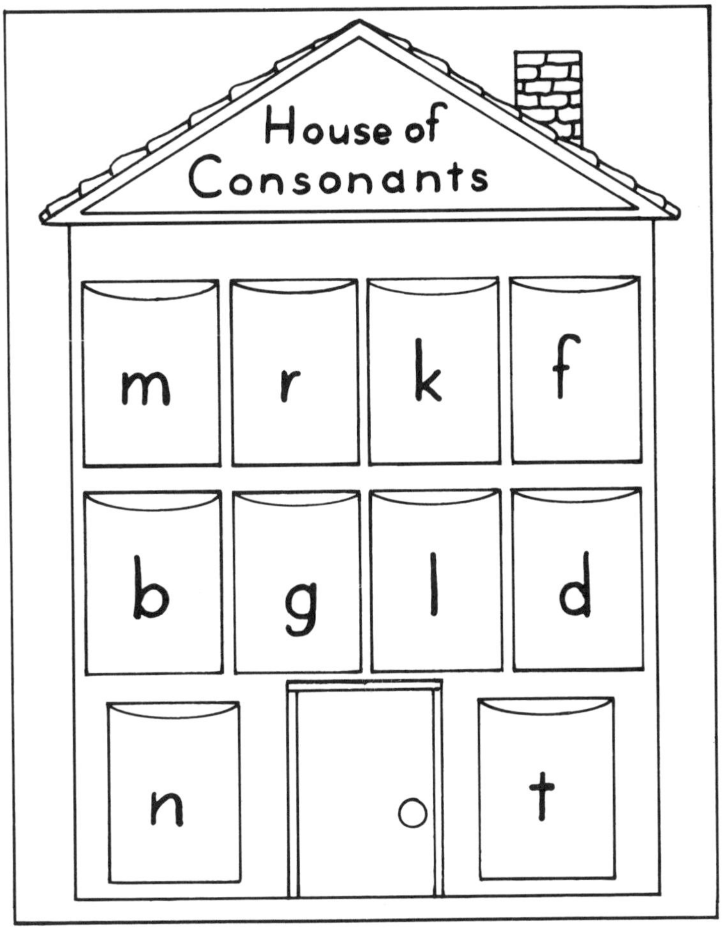

Classifying Sounds

Skill Development: Visual and auditory discrimination of initial or final consonants.

Construction: Cut one piece of colored posterboard sixteen inches by ten inches. Cut another piece sixteen inches by four inches. Use masking tape to attach the smaller piece of posterboard to the bottom of the larger piece so that it forms a pocket. Tape along the sides and the bottom of the smaller piece. Attach library card pockets to the top piece of the board. Write each consonant on cards and paper clip them to the card pocket. This way the consonant may be changed when needed. Use pictures cut from old workbooks or picture books or *Ideal* pegboard picture cards to insert in the pockets.

Utilization: Students are asked to look at the picture, identify it, and then insert it in the correct card pocket.

Initial Consonant Picture Folder

Skill Development: Visual and auditory perception of initial consonants.

Construction: Cut large pieces of posterboard 10″ x 12″. From these pieces of board, cut large three-inch-wide letters. On each letter, mount pictures with the same sound as the letter. To make the accordion folder, cut pieces of board and lay them flat on a table about 1/8 inch apart. Tape them together with strips of masking tape. Mount the letters on the folder. The folder should now be able to stand alone.

Utilization: First, the students should identify each picture pasted on the letters. Then, the students may practice writing the letters, and writing words beginning with each letter. They may also write the corresponding lowercase letters. The teacher may wish to make a duplicate set of letters that are not attached to a folder. Each student should choose a letter, take it to his seat, and trace the outline of the letter with his finger.

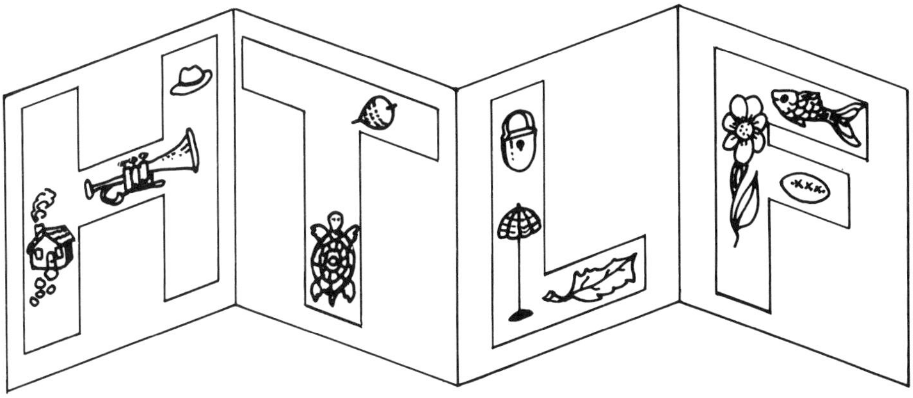

Crossword Puzzles

Skill Development: Initial consonants and word meaning.

Construction: Draw the outline of an object on a piece of 22″ x 28″ posterboard. All the words that are to go into the puzzle should begin with the same sound as the object. Write the clues for *across* and *down* close to the crossword puzzle. Print the appropriate letters on colored cubical blocks or on colored pieces of posterboard.

Utilization: Have two students work together to read the directions for the puzzle, pairing a slow reader with an accelerated reader. If both pupils have difficulty reading the directions, the teacher or teacher's aide may read to the students. Direct the children to find the letters that spell each word correctly and to place them in the correct spaces. Continue working across and down until the puzzle is completed.

B

Across

1. Children ride to school on this.
2. We read from these.

Down

1. Something used to build a playhouse.
2. You hit the ball with this.

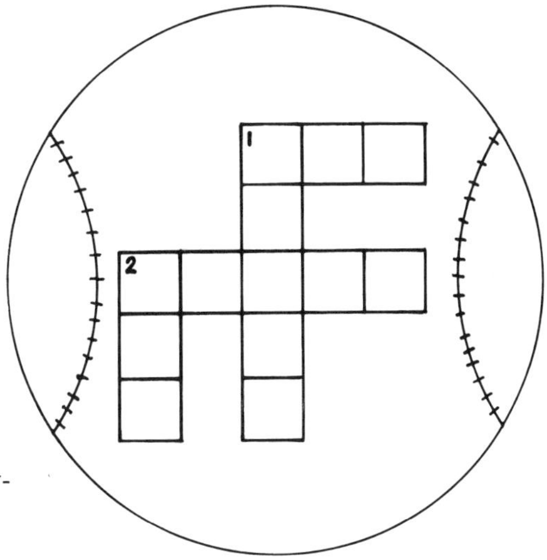

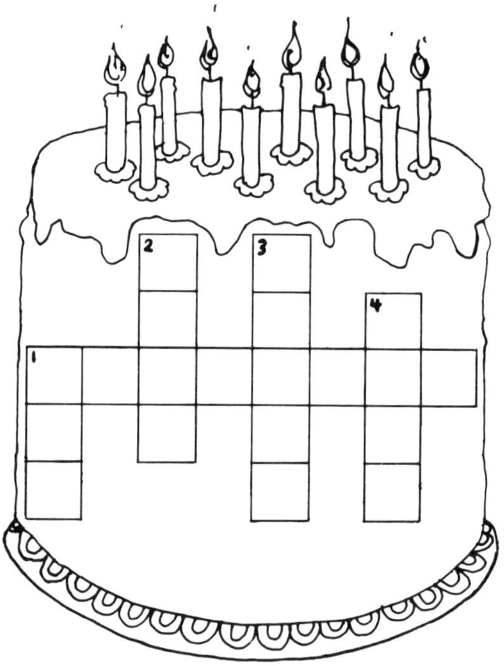

C

Across

1. Tells the months of the year.

Down

1. A small furry animal, often a household pet.
2. Lacking heat; opposite of hot.
3. Very sweet and good to eat.
4. Something that is baked, has candles, and is eaten at a birthday party.

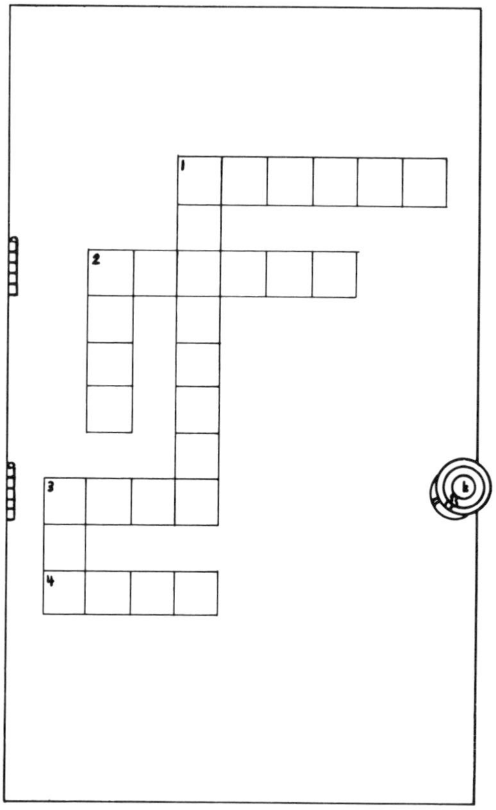

D

Across

1. After dinner Mother washes these.
2. Someone to go to when you are sick.
3. What we go through when we go into the house.
4. Opposite of up.

Down

1. Christmas comes in this month.
2. Without light.
3. Another name for father.

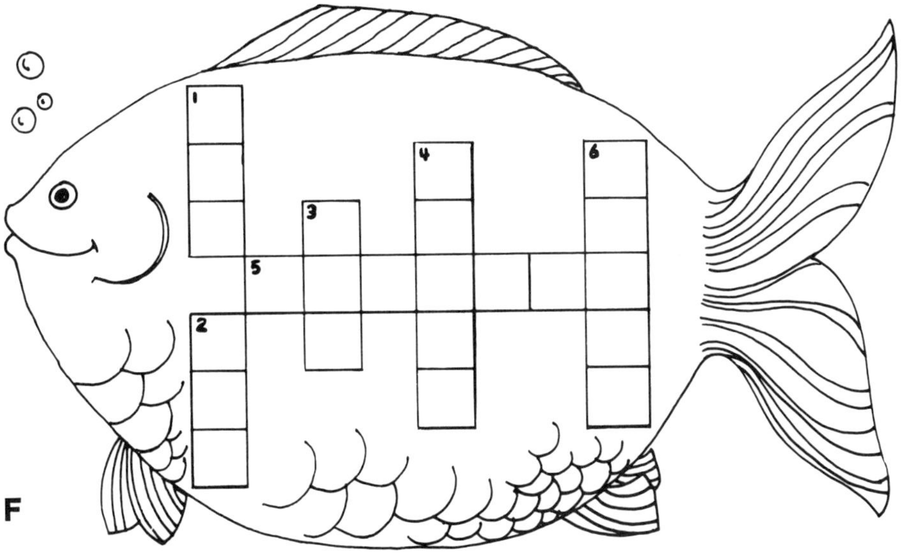

F

Across

5. Objects used when pouring liquids through narrow openings.

Down

1. A small wild animal with a long tail and pointed ears.
2. The opposite of near.
3. The hair on an animal.
4. Anything that makes you laugh.
6. What boxers hit with.

G

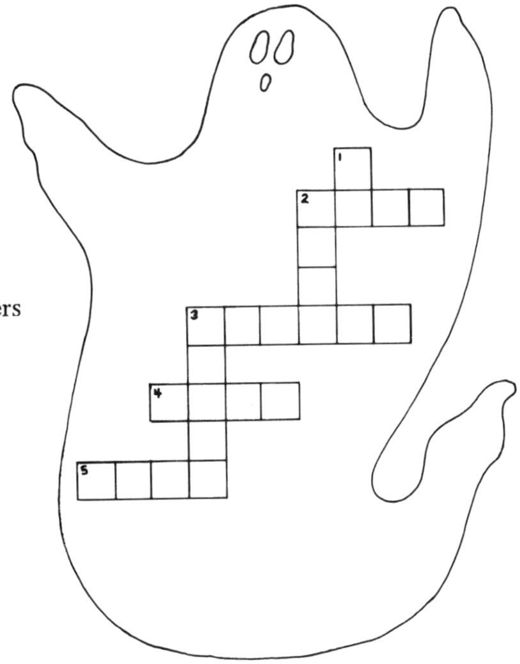

Across

2. The opposite of bad.
3. A piece of ground where flowers or vegetables are grown.
4. A horned animal sometimes found on farms.
5. Something given; a present.

Down

1. To depart; to leave.
2. A bright yellow metal used to make jewelry.
3. The spirit of a dead person.

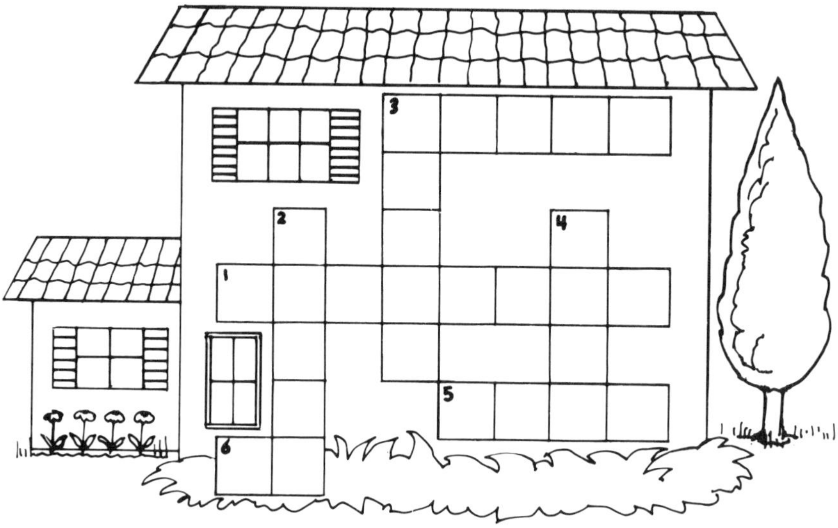

H

Across

1. A place for sick people.
3. A large animal to ride.
5. To keep from being seen.
6. A boy or man.

Down

2. What we live in.
3. The opposite of sad.
4. The part of the body at the end of an arm.

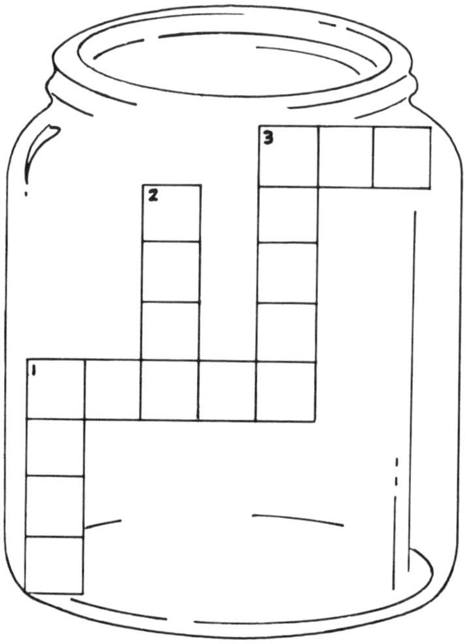

J

Across

1. A word meaning cheerful.
3. A container made from glass.

Down

1. To come together; to unite.
2. A prison.
3. Something that is good with peanut butter on bread.

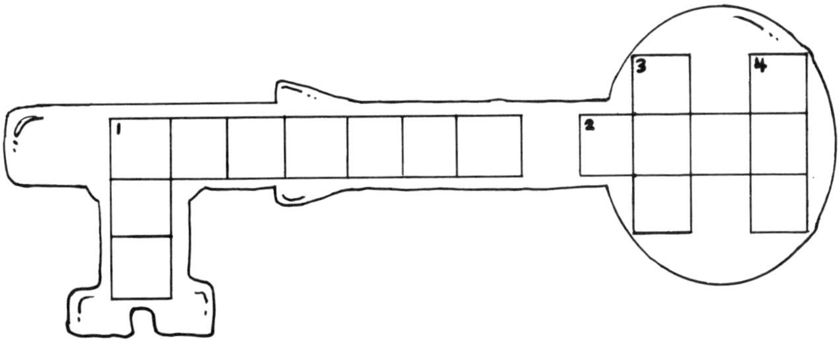

K

Across

1. A room in which cooking is done.
2. Something children like to fly in the wind.

Down

1. A boy's name.
3. To fool or tease.
4. Used to open a lock.

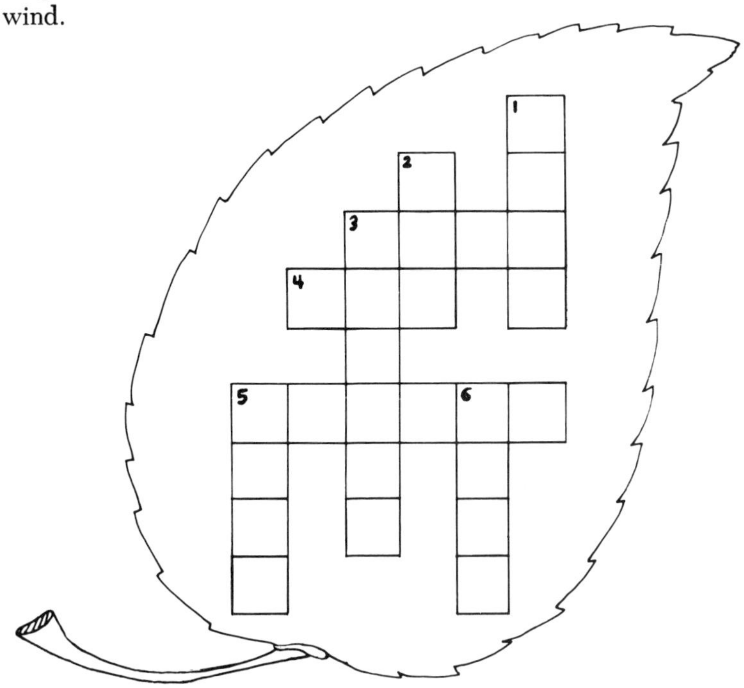

L

Across

3. To see.
4. This is used for walking.
5. The opposite of big.

Down

1. A place to go swimming and boating.
2. Part of a dead tree.
3. Something you write to another person.
5. A part of a tree.
6. Something used to fasten a door.

M

Across

1. A short way of saying mother.
2. What a band plays.
3. A female parent; opposite of father.
5. A long-tailed animal smaller than an ape.

Down

1. A very high hill.
4. More than one man.
5. Something white that we drink.

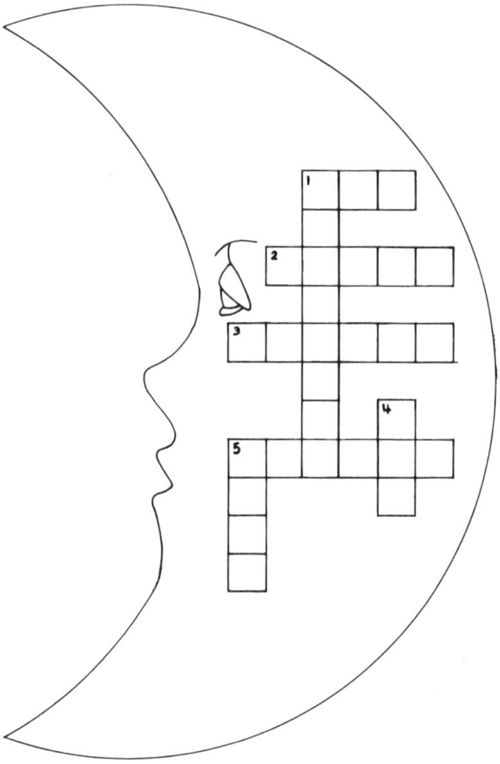

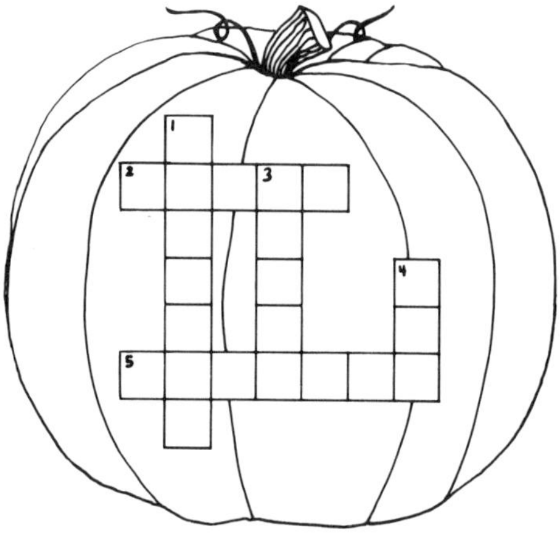

P

Across

2. A young dog.
5. What we make with our crayons or paints.

Down

1. A large, round, orange vegetable used to make a jack-o'-lantern.
3. One who flies an airplane.
4. A good dessert made with a crust.

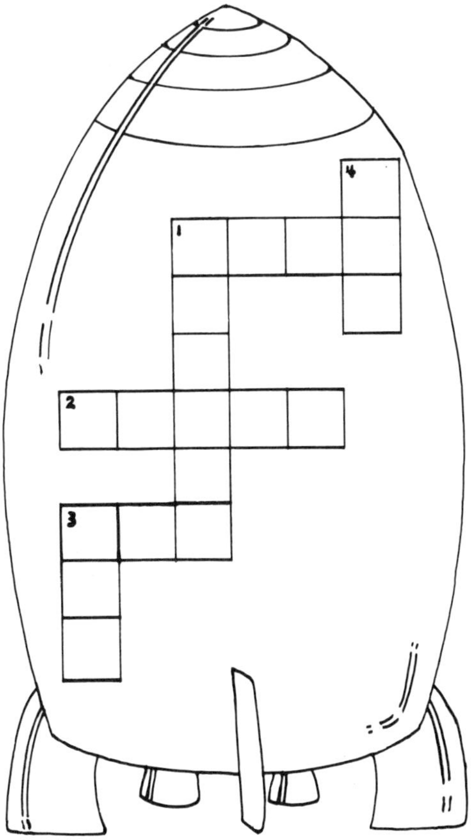

R

Across

1. A heavy cord used for tying.
2. A bird with a red breast.
3. An animal like a mouse but larger.

Down

1. A small, furry animal with long ears.
3. A floor covering.
4. One of the primary colors.

S

Across

3. The day before Sunday.
5. To use needle and thread.

Down

1. A bitter taste; not sweet.
2. When you are not happy.
4. Free from danger.

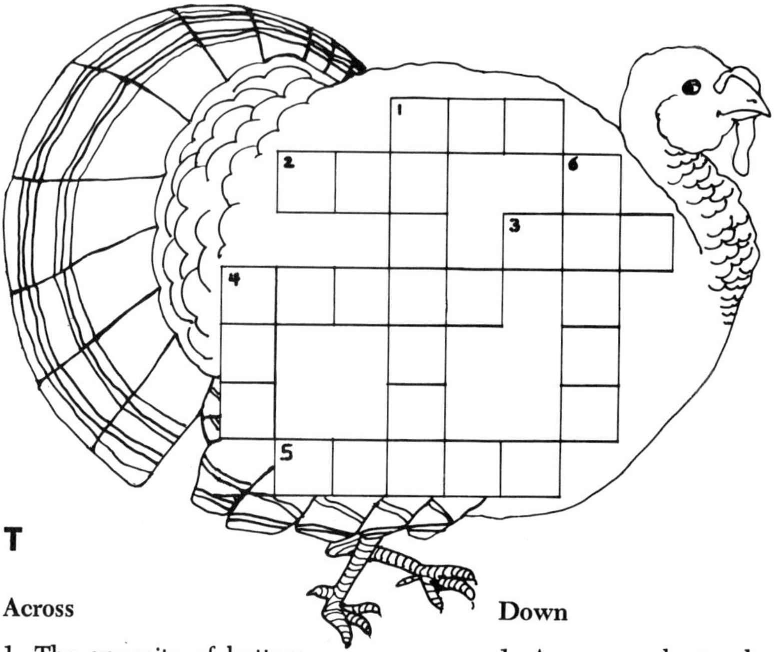

T

Across

1. The opposite of bottom.
2. A part of the foot.
3. A drink made with hot water and a little bag.
4. To feel.
5. Not rested.

Down

1. A person who teaches school.
4. Same as also; to, two, ________.
6. An Indian house.

V

Across

1. A soft, smooth type of cloth.
2. A small town in the country.
3. A sleeveless jacket worn by men.

Down

4. A plant that is used for food; beets, carrots, and beans, for example.

W

Across

1. If you want something, you make a ________.
2. An opening in a wall to let in air and light.

Down

1. The coldest season of the year.
2. To stay in one place; to delay.
3. The part of a bird used for flying.

Consonant Clock

Skill Development: Visual and auditory perception of initial or final consonants.

Construction: Draw a fifteen-inch circle on posterboard, tagboard, or showboard. Letters may be printed or made from felt, sandpaper, or pipe cleaners. Glue or staple the letters to the clock in a circular arrangement. Attach the clock hand with a paper fastener.

Utilization: The student spins the hand on the clock and then gives a word beginning or ending with the sound on which the hand stops.

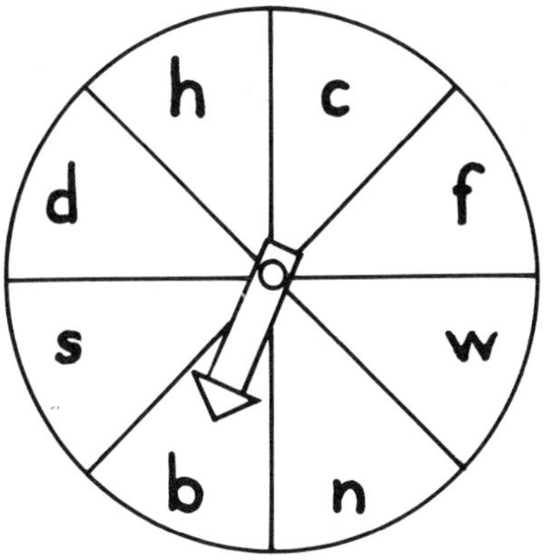

Target Game

Skill Development: Visual and auditory perception of initial, final, and medial consonants.

Construction: Use fourteen-ply showboard and draw a green circle twenty inches in diameter, a white circle fifteen inches in diameter, a yellow circle ten inches in diameter, and a red circle five inches in diameter. Glue the white circle to the middle of the green circle. Glue the yellow circle to the middle of the white circle. Glue the red circle (bulls-eye) to the middle of the yellow circle. On the circles, print the consonant sounds that are most needed. Separate each letter with a line. Use a table easel to hold the target.

Utilization: The student throws a dart and gives the appropriate initial, final, or medial sound for the letter that he hits. Older students may be asked to spell a complete word. Scoring is as follows:

green area, 2 points	yellow area, 4 points
white area, 3 points	bulls-eye, 5 points

Note: This activity is suggested for older, well-adjusted pupils.

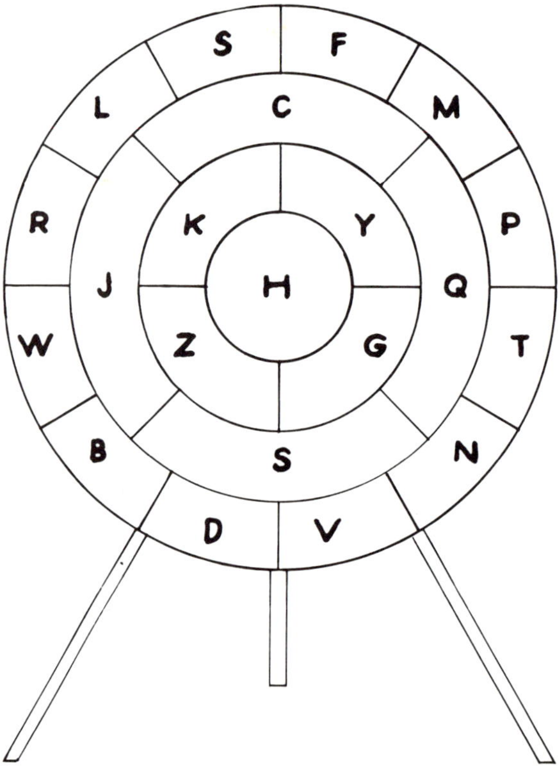

Spelling Tic-tac-toe

Skill Development: Hearing initial, medial, and final sounds.

Construction: Cut a piece of showboard 14″ x 14″. Divide the card into nine sections. Paste a picture in each section. Make seven cards of Xs and seven cards of zeros.

Utilization: The game is played like tic-tac-toe. That is, one of the two players must get a straight line vertically, horizontally, or diagonally before he wins the game. Each player must spell the word represented by the pictures correctly before he can put an X or a zero in the square.

Going to School

Skill Development: Initial and final consonants.

Construction: Use heavy showboard 28″ x 44″ for the background. On this board draw a house and a road that leads from the house to a school. The road should have twenty-two spaces. Use construction paper to make several pairs of shoes of different colors. The object of the game is for each player to move the shoes from the house toward the school, following the directions given at each station. Make a deck of cards numbered from one to twenty-three.

Utilization: Place the cards face down in front of the players. A player must draw from the deck of cards to know how many steps to take. If he draws card 10, he would move ten spaces and follow the direction in the space where he lands. In this case, he would name some foods that begin with *M*. If he could not name foods that begin with *M*, he would return to his original position on the board. If he drew card 23, he would win the game, because that card would put him at school. If he draws card 12, he would go back home and start the game over. As many as six children may play this game. Each child draws a card in turn and places it in a central discard pile. When the cards are used up, they should be reshuffled. The game continues until at least three children reach school.

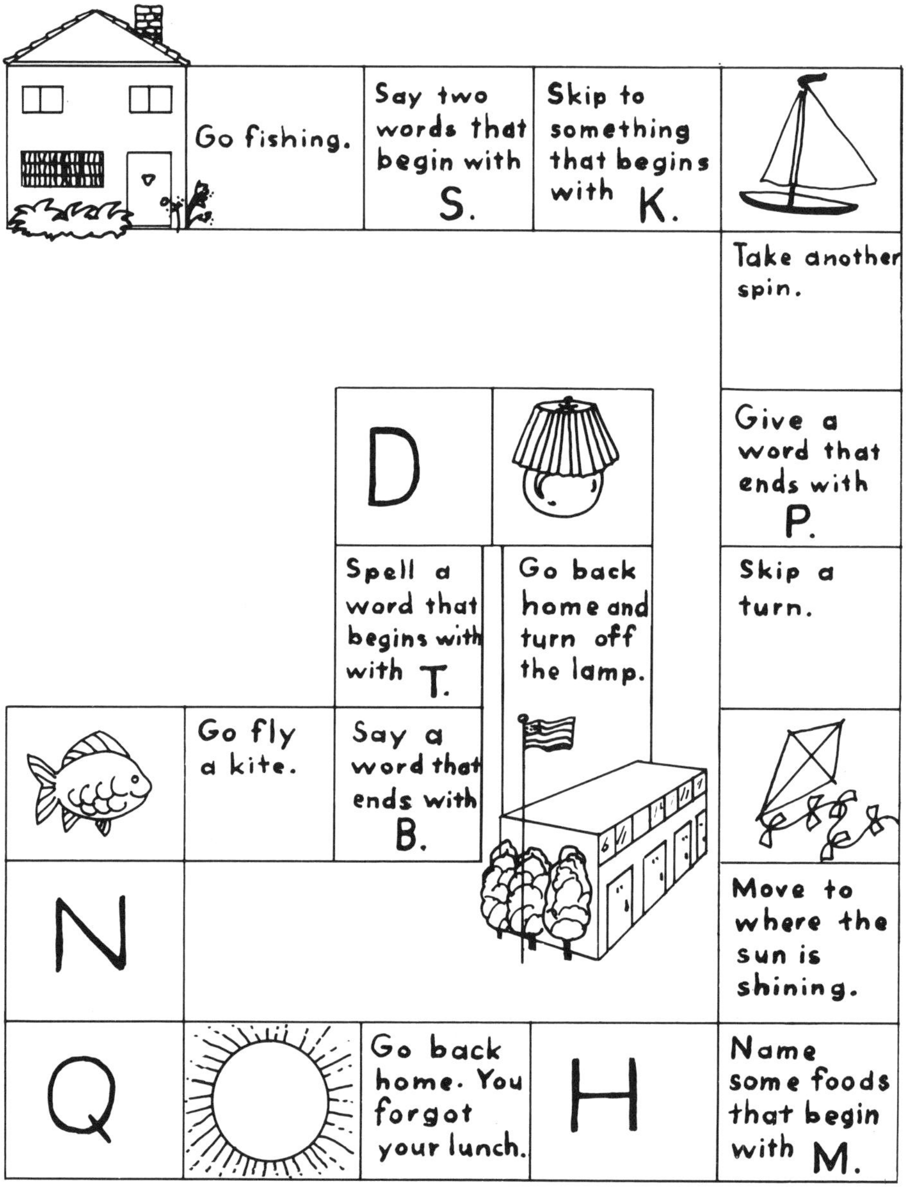

Consonant Baseball

Skill Development: Initial or final consonants.

Construction: Use a large piece of showboard 28″ x 22″ for background. Cut four 15″ x 4″ strips to form the diamond. To make the bases, cut five-inch circles and place one at each corner of the diamond. Make several circles and label them with the consonants that need most practice. Attach the circles with paper fasteners so that they may be changed.

Utilization: The first batter of Team A starts with the letter in the box at first base. He must give a word beginning or ending with the letter. He must do so for each base in order to score a run. If he misses on any base, he is out. When a team has three outs, the other team comes to bat. Change the letters frequently.

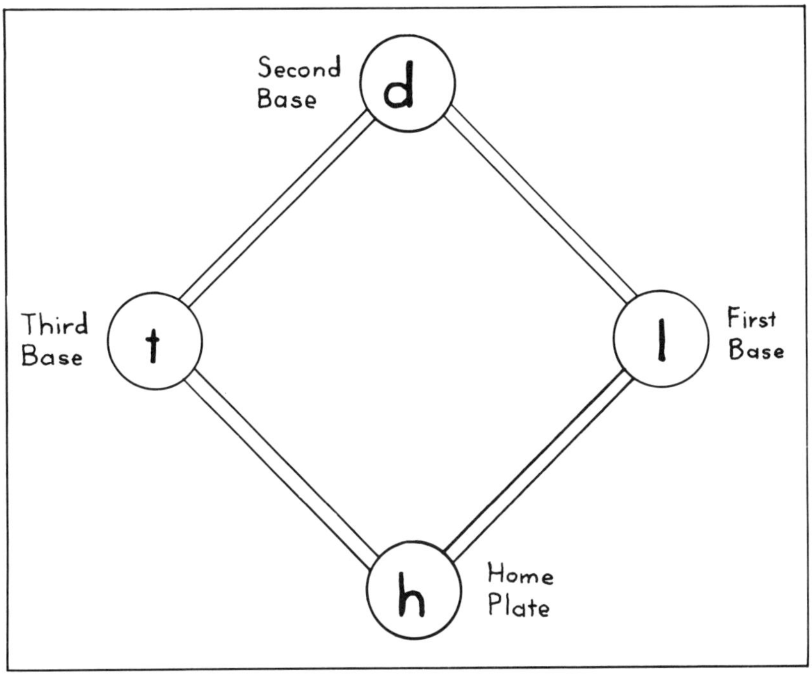

Matching Pictures with Words

Skill Development: Initial consonants.

Construction: Attach pictures and matching words to heavy cardboard. Put the pictures on the left side of the board and the words on the right side, but not in the same order. Attach yarn to the right of each picture. Punch a hole to the left of each word.

Utilization: The student matches the word with the picture by taking the yarn that is opposite the picture and inserting it in the hole next to the word. *Variation:* Use posterboard to make a card holder. Ask the student to match the words with the pictures by placing them next to each other.

Your Move

Skill Development: Initial or final consonants.

Construction: Measure a piece of red showboard 16″ x 20″. Cut two-inch squares from yellow or white bristol board. Paste the squares on the board in alternate positions to form a checkerboard. On each yellow square write two consonants. Write one consonant in an upside-down position so that both players see the same letters.

Utilization: The game is played like checkers. A player can jump over another man but must be able to give a word that begins or ends with that letter before he is allowed to move into a space. Players are only required to give words for empty spaces. A player may not move into a space that is already occupied. Painted bottle caps, cubical blocks, buttons, beans, or pieces of cardboard may be used for tokens.

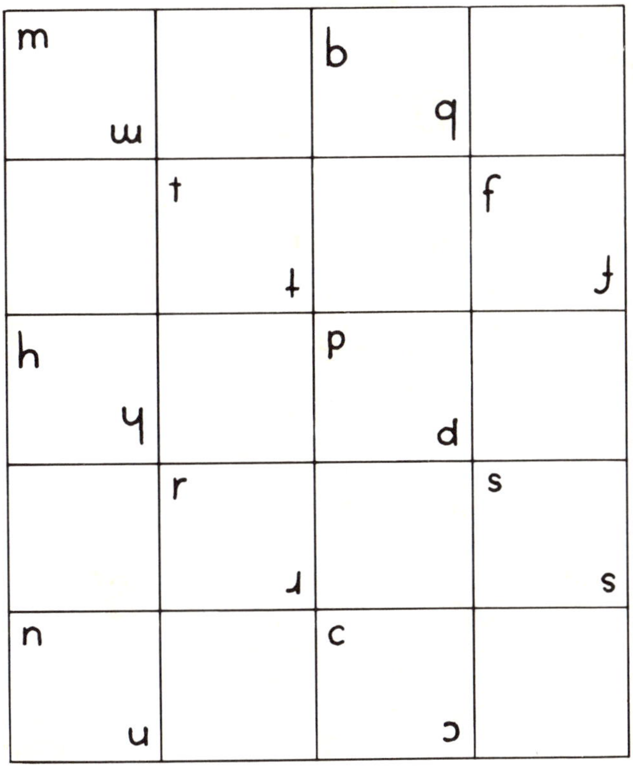
m
b
t
f
h
p
r
s
n
c

Chapter 6

VISUAL-AUDITORY PERCEPTION OF LONG AND SHORT VOWEL SOUNDS

Many classroom and reading teachers agree that teaching vowel sounds to youngsters is one of the most difficult, if not the most difficult, task involved in the teaching of reading. Their reason for this conclusion is that vowel combinations have varying sounds in many different words. Most teachers would prefer to teach long vowels before short vowels because long vowels say their name and are therefore easier for pupils to master. Conversely, short vowels do not say their name and are therefore more difficult to remember. Most teachers use a picture clue to help pupils remember the sound that short vowels make. The most commonly used clues are *apple* for short *a*, *elephant* for short *e*, *Indian* for short *i*, *octopus* for short *o*, and *umbrella* for short *u*.

Since a teacher must spend a great deal of time teaching vowel sounds, she must use a variety of multimedia equipment and worksheets. The games in Chapter 6 give the teacher additional media to use in developing long and short vowel skills.

Silent "E"

Skill Development: Long vowel words ending with silent *e*.

Construction: Use 10″ x 2″ strips of white or manila tagboard. Crease the strips about 2½ inches from the right end. Write the short vowel word to the left of the crease. Write *e* to the right of the crease. Fold the strip along the crease. When the strip is folded, the short vowel word shows. When the *e* on the fold is visible, the letters on the strip spell a long vowel word.

Utilization: These strips may be used for practice after the teacher has introduced the skill for words ending in silent *e*. Some words that may be used for this game are listed on the next page.

hop—hope
pin—pine
hat—hate
cap—cape
tub—tube
fat—fate
kit—kite

pal—pale
grip—gripe
slid—slide
tam—tame
mad—made
mop—mope
dim—dime

cut—cute
cub—cube
mat—mate
not—note
scrap—scrape
slat—slate
fin—fine

fad—fade
bit—bite
rip—ripe
man—mane
rot—rote
tap—tape
Tim—time

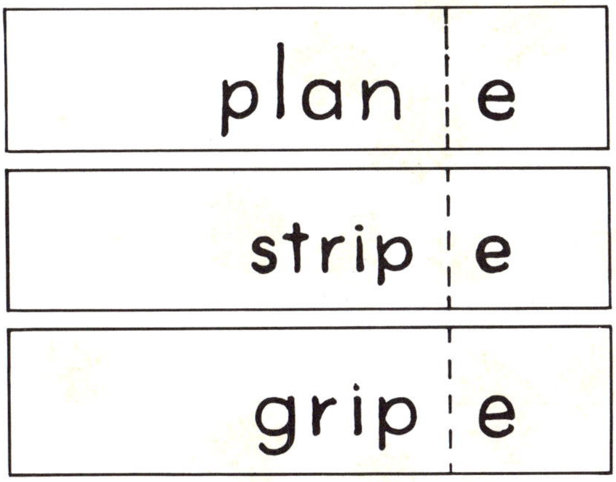

Walking Vowels

Purpose: Helps students remember the vowels.

Construction: Use 11″ x 7″ showboard. Cut large black letters (lower-case) and attach to the board. Draw stick figures for the rest of the body. Add eyes for expression.

Utilization: These vowel cards may be used as flash cards or bulletin board decoration.

Vowel Throw-board

Skill Development: Recalling words that contain short vowel sounds.

Construction: Draw the face of a clown or an animal on a 25″ x 29″ piece of beaverboard, plywood, or any other durable material. Cut out openings for the mouth, eyes, and ears. Write a vowel near each opening.

Utilization: Assign points for each opening on the face. Stand the board in a slanted position against a chair or a wall. The student may use either a beanbag or a ball for tossing. Each player may toss five bags. If a beanbag goes through an opening, he must give a short vowel word for that vowel. If the word is correct, he scores the designated points. The object of the game is to get the highest score.

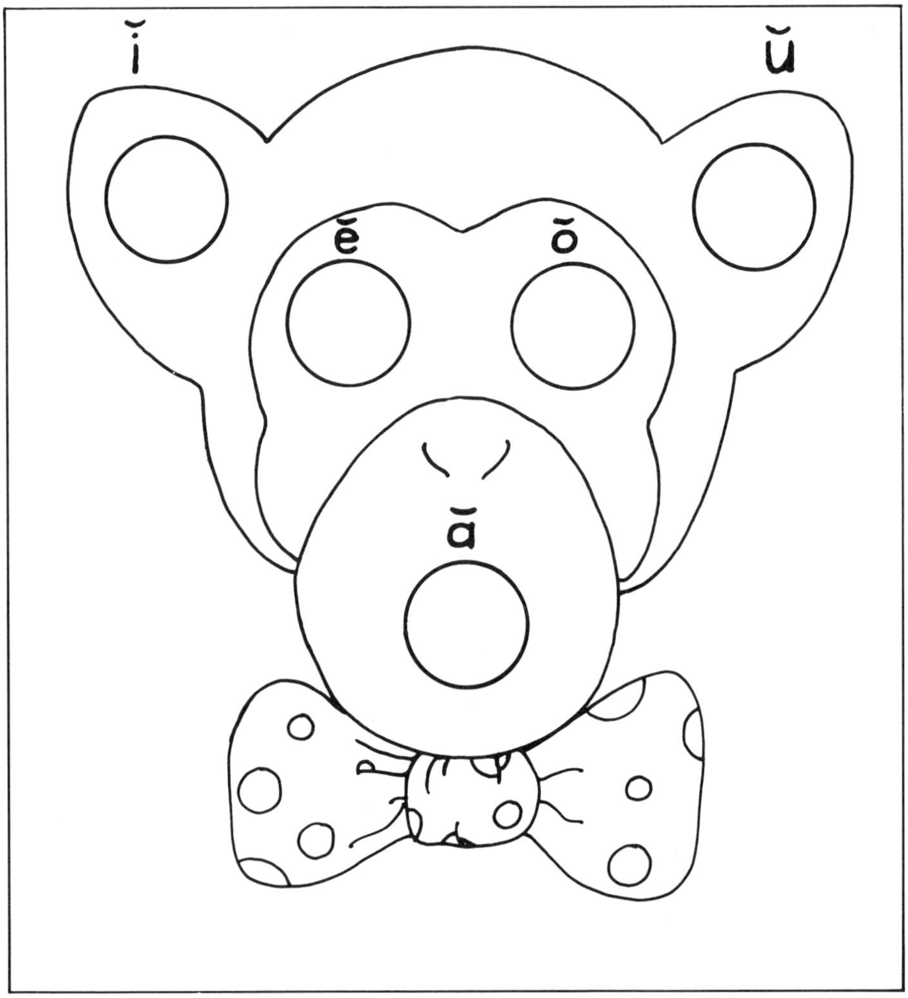

Roll-a-vowel

Skill Development: Use of long or short vowel words.

Construction: Write a vowel on each side of wooden or styrofoam blocks. In the upper right-hand corner of each side, write a number. The six sides would look like this:

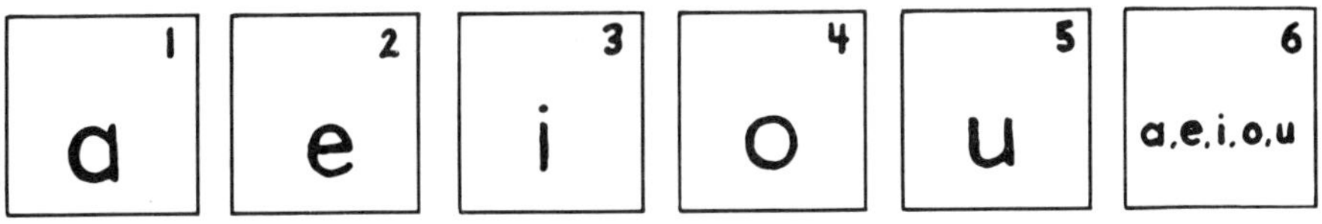

Utilization: Each player rolls five blocks on the floor or on the table and gives a word for the vowels that are facing upward. He should name the vowel in the word and tell if the vowel is long or short. The player has the choice of choosing to use long or short vowel words. For example, if the blocks stopped with *o, a, o, i, u,* facing upwards, the player could say *pot, face, stop, dime, tube.* His total number of points would be 17. If one of the blocks stopped on *all vowels,* he could say *hat, egg, ink, slow,* and *tub.* He would get 6 points for that block if the words and vowels are correct. After each player has rolled the blocks, the scores are added by the teacher or another student. If words and vowels do not correspond correctly, the player does not score. The first player to reach one hundred points wins the game. From two to six children may play the game.

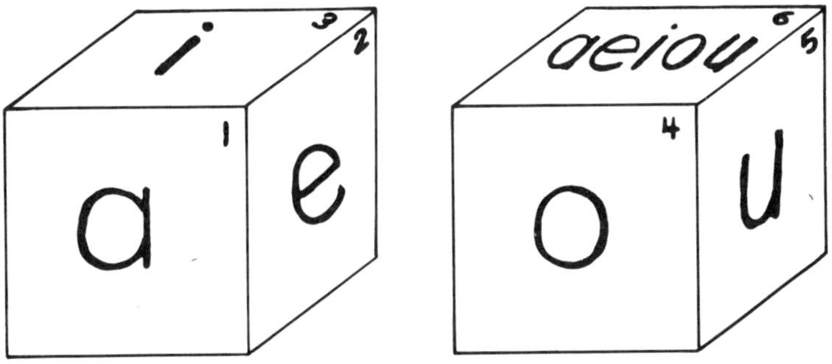

Vowel Bingo

Skill Development: Recognizing words that contain the long sound of *a.*

Construction: Rule twenty-five spaces on several cards. Write a long vowel in the center space and a word in each of the other spaces. Each card should have a different arrangement of the same words. Use pieces of posterboard, bottlecaps, or beans for counters.

Utilization: The game is played like bingo. The player who gets a straight line horizontally, vertically, or diagonally wins the game. The winner may call the next game.

nail	bail	day	main	hay
stay	clay	mail	way	sail
trail	rain	ā	faint	brain
say	gray	lay	chain	pray
daisy	train	pail	tray	bay

Syllable Game

Skill Development: Identification and pronunciation of words with like syllables.

Construction: Write fifty-two compound words and words having prefixes and suffixes on 3″ x 5″ cards. Be sure that at least two of the cards match (confuse-concern), (peaceable-washable), (blacksmith-blackjack).

Utilization: Four players are the maximum suggested for the game. Each player receives five cards. Stack the other cards in the center of the table. Each time a player can match two words with like syllables, he gets three points. He gets an additional point for each word he can pronounce correctly. For example, if he were to match *review* and *rewrite,* he would get three points. If he could pronounce both words, he would get two more points. If he could pronounce only one of the words, he would get one additional point. When all of the cards from the stack are used, the players draw from each other until all cards are matched. The highest scorer wins the game.

Silent Letter Chart

Skill Development: Pronouncing words with silent letters, hard and soft *c,* and *g* and *gu* sounds.

Construction: Cut several pieces of 9″ x 22″ showboard. Mount a picture at the top of the board as a clue to pronouncing the words. For example, a picture of a knight is a good clue for words beginning with the silent *k*. List several words on these cards. Emphasize the *kn* combination by writing those two letters in a vivid color. After all cards are completed, bind them with large loose-leaf rings.

Utilization: Use the cards for practice and drill.

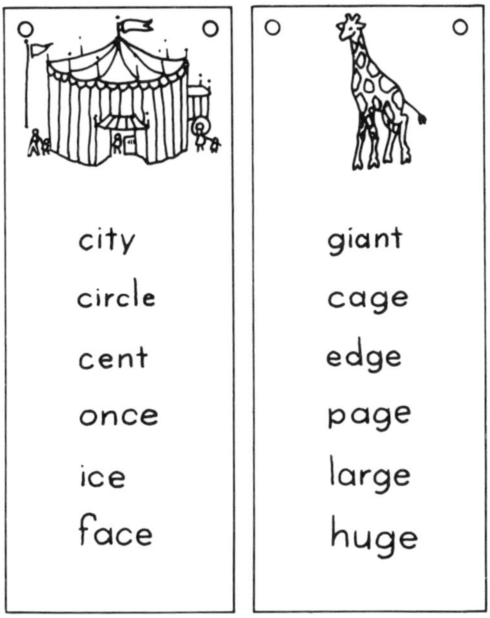

Short Sound of "U"

Skill Development: Blending or pronouncing short *u* words.

Construction: On 3″ x 9″ manila cards, write words that contain short *u*. Write all of the letters in black except the letter *u*. The color helps the student to remember that the *u* is short. Use a 9″ x 12″ piece of manila tag to construct a pocket to hold the words when they're not being used. Write *Short Vowel U* on the front of the pocket.

Utilization: Ask a student to pronounce the words. Encourage him to use the dictionary to define words that he doesn't know.

Prefix Puzzle

Skill Development: Practice on words having prefixes.

Construction: Write words that use a prefix on 3″ x 9″ manila cards. Leave one inch between the prefix and the root of the word. Draw a wide zigzag line to divide the prefix from the root. Cut the zigzag line down the middle so that the line shows on both pieces of the card. Make a folder to hold the puzzle.

Utilization: Students are to fit the parts together to make a complete word. They should be able to use the word in a sentence.

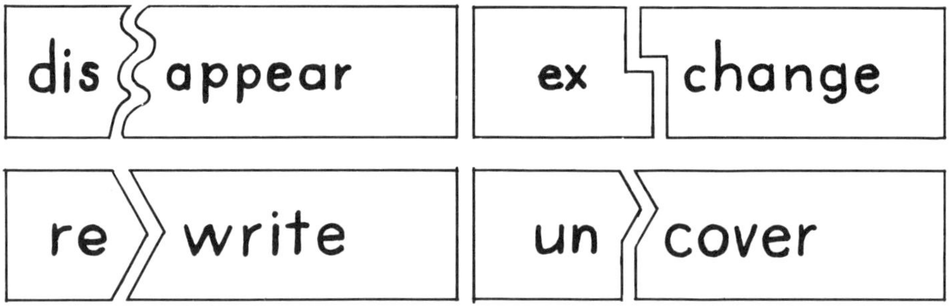

Blending Cards

Skill Development: Blending initial sounds with long vowels.

Construction: On 4″ x 6″ cards, write a group of words (word family) that have the same sound except for the initial sound—bake, cake, rake, etc. Bind the words with a loose-leaf ring.

Utilization: Introduce long *a* to the students. Use these cards to give them practice in working with the long vowel *a*.

Red Wagon

Skill Development: Recognition of short and long vowel words.

Construction: From red fourteen-ply showboard, cut two pieces of board 17″ x 7″. Cut two wheels 5½″ in diameter. Cut a handle that is 1″ wide and 7½″ long. Staple the two pieces of 17″ x 7″ boards at the bottom and at both sides, leaving an opening at the left side for the handle. Staple the handle and wheels to the wagon. Do not staple the top of the wagon. Cut five cards 4″ x 10″. These words should be written on each card:

w	a	g	o	n
web	am	gap	over	nag
with	at	gas	open	nut
wag	as	gun	old	nap
wig	add	gum	oak	nest
wish	ask	glass	oat	numb
wick	ant	grass	oath	nickel
wind	apple	grin	on	number
wing	aid	grub	ocean	nurse

Utilization: A student should take one of the cards from the wagon. When he can pronounce the *w* words, he may take the next card containing *a* words. Have the students choose another word that is the name of a vehicle, such as *boat* or *train*. Ask them to write words for each letter.

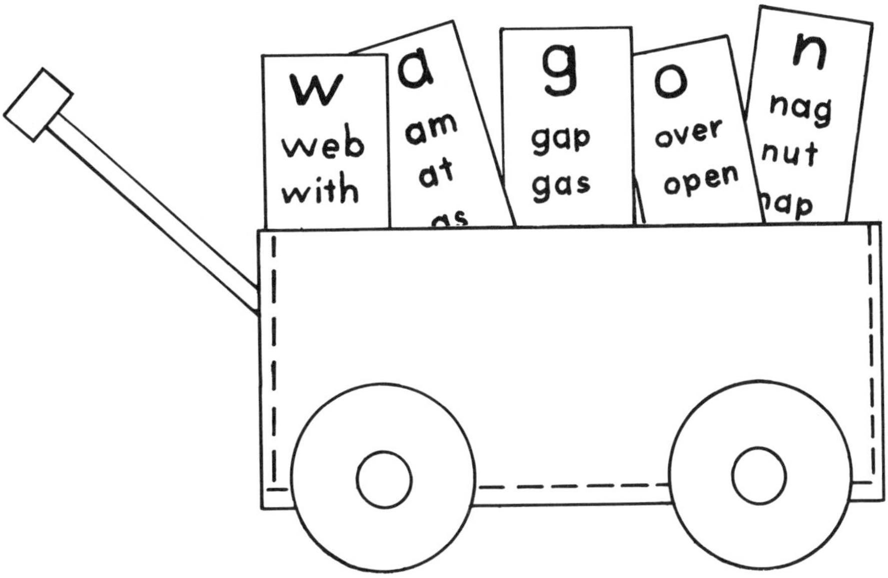

Vowel Detective

Skill Development: Short vowels and word meanings.

Construction: Draw the outline of a large magnifying glass. Make the circular part seven inches in diameter and the handle seven inches long. Divide the face of the magnifying glass into sixteen parts. Write in short vowel words that need reviewing. Make small cards that contain the meaning of each word.

Utilization: Instead of calling the word itself, the teacher reads the meaning of the word. The student must cover the word, and the game proceeds like bingo.

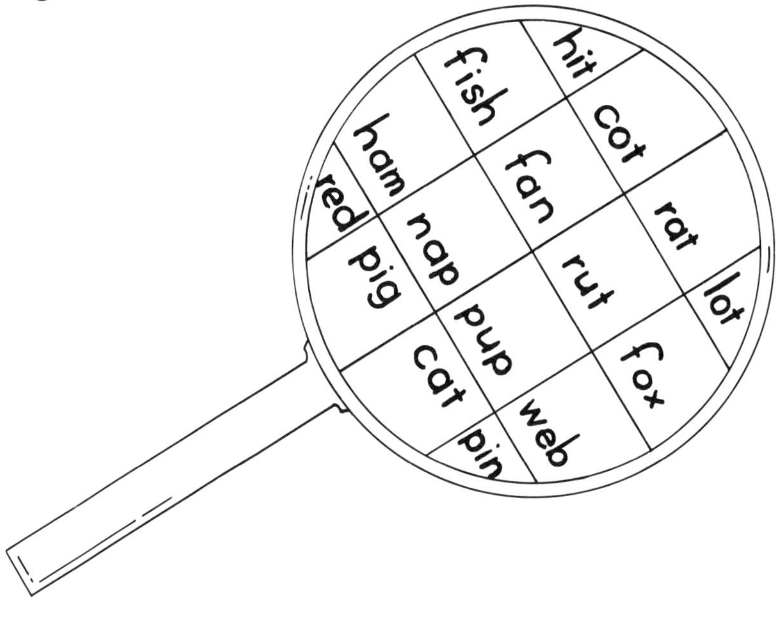

Vowel Pocket

Skill Development: Auditory and visual discrimination of short *i* and short *e*.

Construction: Use 22″ x 14″ posterboard. Fold the bottom part of the board upward to form a four-inch pocket. Then fold the board in half so that it opens like a book. Staple the pocket of the folder in the middle and at the left and right edges. Then divide the right pocket in half using colored tape. Use the same tape as a border on each side of the folder. Write short *i* words at the top of the left side of the folder. Write short *e* words at the top of the right side of the folder. Insert short *i* and *e* picture cards in the bottom pocket on the left side of the folder.

Utilization: The object of the game is to pronounce all of the short *i* and *e* words before placing the pictures in the correct pockets on the right side of the folder. Pictures may be cut from old workbooks or magazines and mounted on tagboard. They may also be ordered from local supply companies that service schools.

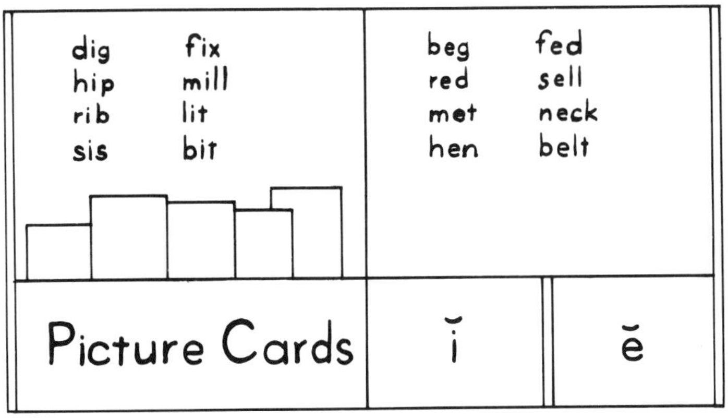

Short and Long Vowels

Skill Development: Recognition and pronounciation of short and long vowel words.

Construction: Cut a fifteen-inch circle from posterboard. Attach a half circle to the bottom to make a pocket to hold word cards. To the top of the circle, attach five library card pockets. Label them with short and long vowel sounds. Print words that have long or short vowel sounds on cards, one word to a card, and put them in the lower pocket. *Variation:* This activity may also be used to give practice with the long and short sound of the same vowel. In this variation, picture cards should be used instead of word cards.

Utilization: The student chooses a word card or a picture card from the large pocket and inserts it into the correct card pocket.

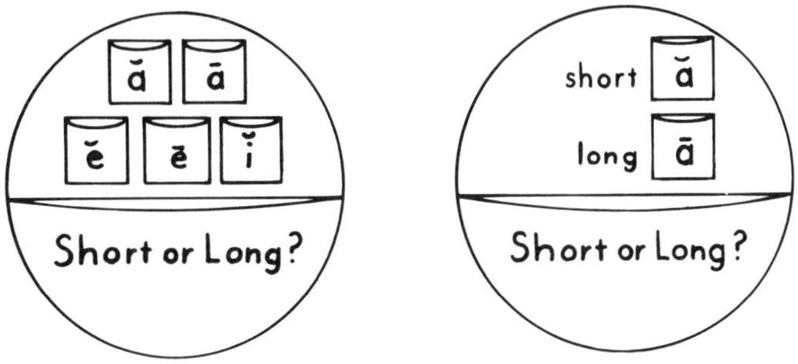

Short Sound of "E"

Skill Development: Ability to blend short *e* words.

Construction: On 3″ x 9″ cards, write words that contain short *e*. Write the vowel *e* in color to emphasize the sound. Construct a folder or pocket to hold the word cards when not in use. Paste a large *ĕ* on the front of the container.

Utilization: The student pronounces, spells, and defines each word in the folder.

Clarence the Clown

Skill Development: Initial consonants, vowels, suffixes, synonyms, or oral language development.

Construction: Mount your favorite clown on a large board or on a bulletin board so that it is easily accessible to the students. Make several small pockets or two large pockets to hold pictures or word cards containing vowels, blends, prefixes, suffixes, etc.

Utilization: One student or a small group of students may practice classifying or pronouncing the pictures or words after the skill has been introduced by the teacher.

Vowel Scrambles

Skill Development: Word meaning and recognition of long or short vowel words.

Construction: On 2″ x 6″ cards, scramble the letters of short or long vowel words. Put a clue on the back of each card. Use long white envelopes to hold the word cards.

Utilization: The student takes a card from the envelope, looks at the clue, and unscrambles the word. He then tells if the vowel is long or short. For example, if the word *skate* appeared, he would say, "The *a* is long and the *e* is silent."

udrm	a toy
kucd	abird

Short Vowel Match-board

Skill Development: Visual-auditory perception of short or long vowel sounds.

Construction: Fold a piece of 22″ x 11″ posterboard in half so that it makes a 22″ x 5½″ standing board. Divide the front of the board into five equal squares. In each square, place a picture of each vowel sound. The vowels should not be in sequential order. Write vowel words on 2″ x 4″ cards. Put a library card pocket inside the folder board to hold the word cards when not in use. Attach pieces of masking tape inside each end of the board to keep it in a stable position.

Utilization: Two students may use this activity. Place the board on a table in a standing position so that it can be seen by both players. The word cards are divided equally among both players. The players take turns matching each card under the appropriate picture. For example, the word card *glass* would be placed under the picture of the cat. The word card *frog* would be placed under the picture of the clock.

House of Vowels

Skill Development: Auditory and visual perception of short vowel sounds.

Construction: Draw and cut out a large house, approximately 25″ x 20″. Draw in a door and attach five-inch pockets for holding picture cards.

Utilization: Two or three students may use this game to review their skill with all short vowels. All of the cards should be mixed well in a stack. The students look at the picture cards and insert them in the correct pocket. All short *a* picture cards would be inserted in the first pocket. All short *e* picture cards would be inserted in the fourth pocket, and so on until all picture cards have been inserted.

Vowel Faces

Skill Development: Visual and auditory perception of short and long vowels, vocabulary building, and word meaning.

Construction: Staple together two half-circles twenty inches in diameter to form a large pocket. Insert word cards with a word on the front of the card and the meaning of the word on the back of the card. Leave out the vowel when you spell the word. Make five vowel faces and attach these to the front of the folder.

Utilization: The teacher holds up the definition for the student to read. The student must try to identify the word from the definition. When he has identified the word correctly, have him supply the missing vowel and tell if the vowel is long or short. Then have him reproduce the sound of that vowel.

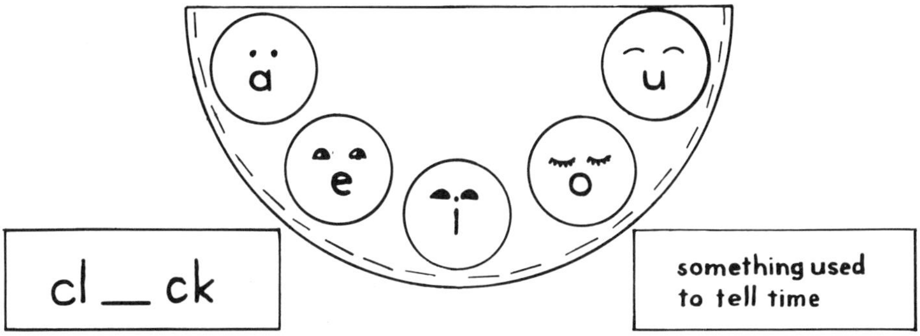

Vowel Charts for the Teacher

Purpose: Introduce short vowels, long vowels, vowels controlled by *r*, diphthongs, and double vowels.

Construction: Cut several pieces of 14″ x 22″ colored posterboard. Mount a picture at the top of each board as a clue to the pronunciation of the words. For example, a picture of an ape gives a clue to the long sound of *a*. It helps if all the *a*'s are written in color while the rest of each word is written in black. The charts may be bound together with large rings.

Utilization: The teacher should first introduce the long *a* on the chalkboard, explaining as she goes. Then use the chart for extra practice and drill. The student may wish to pronounce the words first and then use the words as a spelling lesson, looking up unknown words in the dictionary.

Short a

bag	glad
bat	last
bad	hand
dad	flag
cab	back
map	trap
cat	brass
had	slap
tap	lamp

Long e

eat	green
tree	beast
neat	reach
east	speak
meat	feast
seed	steel
feet	sweet
bean	sheep
weak	speed

Chapter 7

VISUAL-AUDITORY PERCEPTION OF CONSONANT BLENDS

A consonant blend may be defined as a combination of two or three letters that, when joined, make up a single speech sound. The child who is a competent reader is capable of equating the speech sounds with their printed symbols. The student who has great difficulty is the one who sees the word *train* and tries to pronounce the word, using the initial sound *t* and adding *rain*. It is therefore the responsibility of the teacher to give adequate practice with two- and three-letter blends separately so that the student is capable of attacking the word with complete comprehension. An excellent technique for introducing blends is to write words that the student knows, such as *lap* and *cap*, then add the blended sound *clap*. The teacher may wish to modify games and activities from this chapter to use with a particular group of children.

Wh Word Wheel

Skill Development: Visual and auditory perception of the consonant digraph *wh*.

Construction: Use posterboard to cut two circles twelve inches in diameter. Draw the spokes, rim, and hub on one wheel. On this same wheel, make one triangular cut so that the words can show through. Write words that begin with the *wh* sound on the blank wheel. Punch a hole in both wheels and use a paper fastener to attach the blank wheel to the wheel with the triangular cut. As the top wheel is rotated, the student should be able to see one word at a time.

Utilization: Ask a student to turn the wheel, pronounce each word, and use it in a sentence.

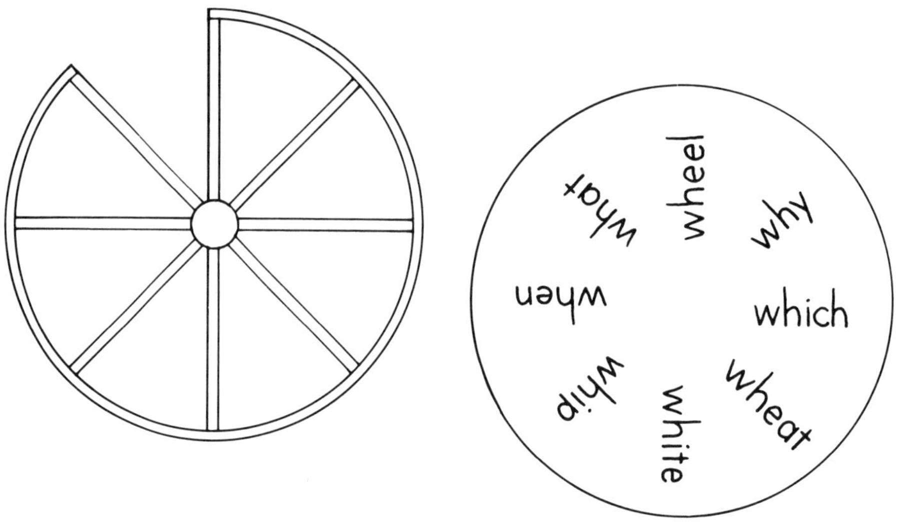

Initial Consonant Blend

Skill Development: Visual and auditory perception of the initial consonant blend *dr*.

Construction: Draw the outline of a dress on a piece of tagboard 10″ x 12″. Cover the dress outline with colorful wallpaper and complete the details with a felt-tip marker. Cut a small slit over the pocket. Cover the back of the slit with a card to form a pocket. Insert words that begin with *dr*.

Utilization: The shape of the dress gives a clue for the beginning sound of each word in the pocket. Ask a child to pronounce each word, use each word in a sentence, and choose a word to illustrate in a picture.

Speech Consonants

Skill Development: Visual and auditory perception of the initial and final consonant digraph *sh.*

Construction: Draw the outline of a shirt on a piece of tagboard 8″ x 12″. Cover the shirt outline with wallpaper or felt. Cut an opening over the pocket. Tape a card to the back of the opening to form a pocket. On small cards, write words that begin and end with the *sh* sound. Insert these small cards in the shirt pocket.

Utilization: The shape of the shirt serves as clue for all the words in the pocket. Ask the student to pronounce the words in the pocket, use the words in sentences, and choose a word to illustrate in a picture.

Show Me

Skill Development: Auditory and visual perception of initial consonant blends.

Construction: Cut two 8″ x 6″ cards from posterboard. Cut a smaller strip 8″ x 2″. Use masking tape to hold the cards together on the bottom and two sides, forming a folder. Leave the top open to hold blend cards. Tape the smaller 8″ x 2″ strip to the bottom front of the folder. The small strip will be used to hold the correct response card. On this small strip, write the words "Show Me." Ask each student to write his own blend cards (bl, st, cl, br, tr, sp, for example). Insert these cards into the folder when not in use.

Utilization: The teacher calls the word *class.* Each student looks through his cards, selects the card *cl,* and puts it in the lower strip holder. The student does not turn the folder toward the teacher until the teacher says "show me." This is an excellent way to evaluate each student individually even though the students are functioning in a group. The teacher should keep notes on the blends that each student missed so that she will know what blends to reteach to each student. This same method may also be used with initial consonants and short and long vowels.

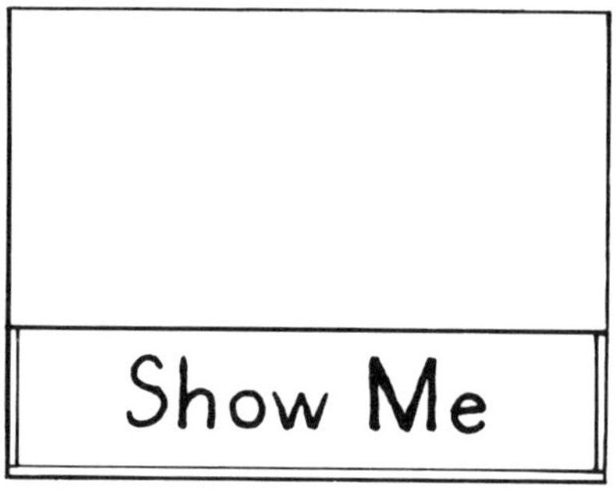

Classifying Blends

Skill Development: Visual perception of initial consonant blends.

Construction: Fold the bottom of a piece of 18″ x 13″ posterboard upward and tape each side to form a pocket. Attach three or four library card pockets near the top. Insert initial consonant blend pictures in the large pocket below.

Utilization: The student takes a picture card from the large pocket and inserts it in the correct library card pocket. For instance, if a student pulled the picture of a *sled,* he would insert it in the *sl* library card pocket.

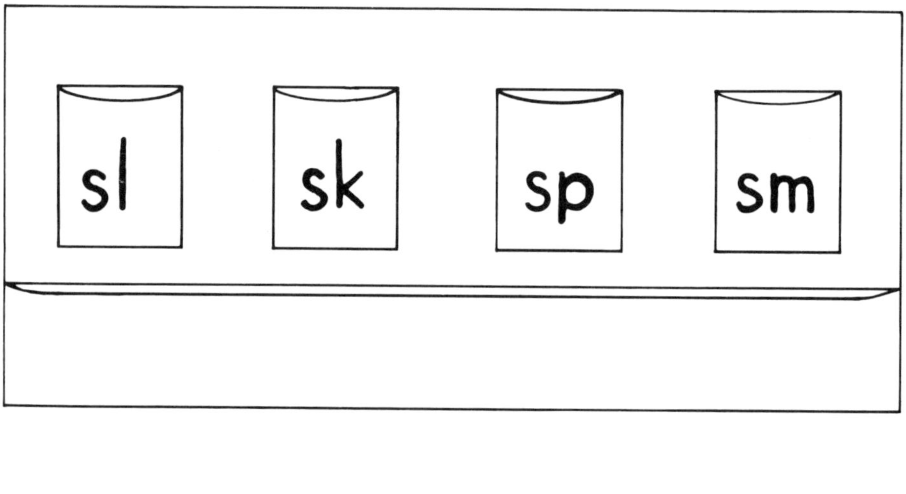

Consonant Blend Match-board

Skill Development: Visual and auditory discrimination of initial consonant blends.

Construction: Cut a 22″ x 11″ piece of posterboard. Fold the board in half so that it will stand up on its own. Mount five pictures on the front of the match-board. Above the pictures, write the name of the activity. On small cards, print words that begin with the same blends as the mounted pictures. Tape a library card pocket to the back of the board to hold the word cards when they are not in use.

Utilization: The student takes the word cards from the back pocket, stands the match-board up, and matches the cards under the appropriate pictures.

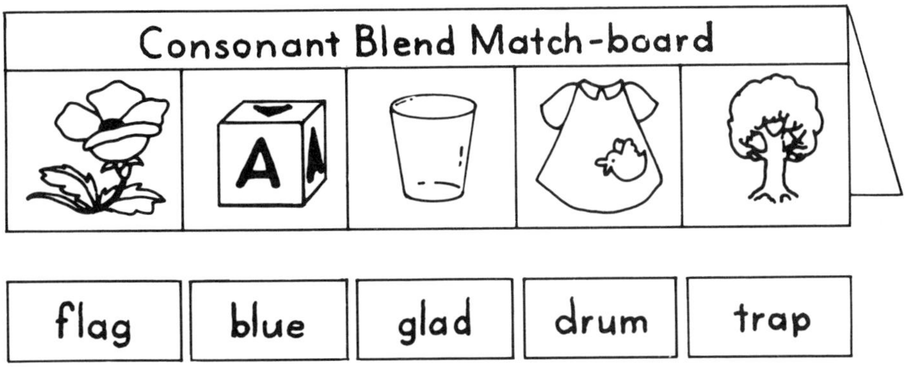

Blend Cards

Skill Development: Visual and auditory perception of initial consonant blends.

Construction: Cut one piece of posterboard 11″ x 11″. Cut a second piece of posterboard 6″ x 6″. Cut the corners off evenly from both pieces of board to form two octagons. Lay the small octagon on top of the larger octagon. Staple the smaller octagon at each angle, a total of eight staples. Between each staple write a consonant blend. Attach a card pocket to hold eight pictures that have been mounted on small pieces of tagboard. Cut the bottom part of the tagboard so that it will slip into the slots.

Utilization: The student looks at the eight pictures and inserts them in the correct slots.

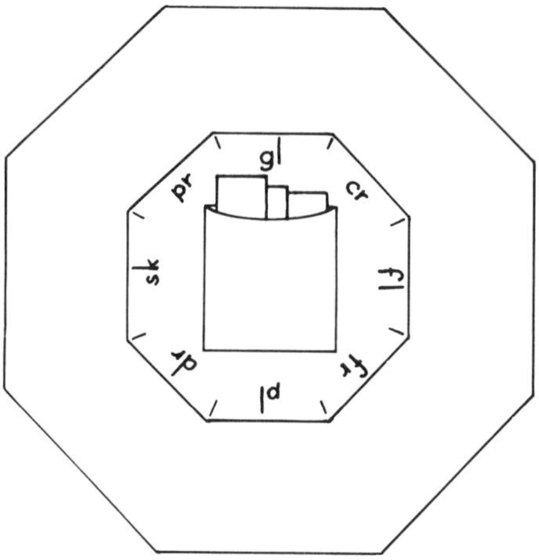

Blend-o

Skill Development: Visual and auditory perception of initial consonant blends.

Construction: Cut several 10″ x 10″ cards from heavy posterboard. Draw horizontal and vertical lines to form twenty-five squares. In each square, write one of the initial consonant blends. Put a picture in the center square. Arrange the blends in a different order on each card.

Utilization: The teacher calls a word and the student covers the corresponding initial blend. If the word *broom* were called, the student would cover *br*. A straight row of correct answers wins the game. In addition, the teacher may ask the winner to uncover each blend, one at a time, and give a word that begins with each blend sound.

bl	st	fr	br	sl
cl	fl	sk	sm	dr
sp	gr		pr	tr
pl	ch	cr	gl	sn
tw	sw	st	sh	sc

Blend Pockets

Skill Development: Recognition of initial consonant blend words.

Construction: Make a pocket folder by cutting a single piece of poster-board 12″ x 10″ and taping a 12″ x 4″ strip to its bottom front. Paste or draw a picture at the top of the folder to give a clue to the words in the pocket.

Utilization: When the pupils can identify the words in the pocket, ask them to sign their names on the back of the folder.

Write-a-sound

Skill Development: Auditory perception of initial consonant blends.

Construction: Make a set of colorful blend pictures, using pictures from old magazines or book jackets.

Utilization: When the teacher shows a picture of a sled, the pupil should write *sl* on his paper. To evaluate progress, the exercise may be repeated orally while each student corrects his written answers.

Concentration

Skill Development: Recalling initial consonant blend words.

Construction: Use a large wooden box approximately 36″ x 36″ x 6″. Make sixteen slots that will accommodate sixteen styrofoam blocks. Write a consonant blend on one end of each block and a number on its opposite end. Use eight consonant blends and sixteen numbers.

Utilization: To play the game, a player calls two numbers and turns the blocks around to show the blends. If the blends match, the player gives a word beginning with the blend, and these blends are left showing. If the player cannot give a word to match the blend, the blends are turned so that only the numbers show. Scores or candy may be given to make the game competitive.

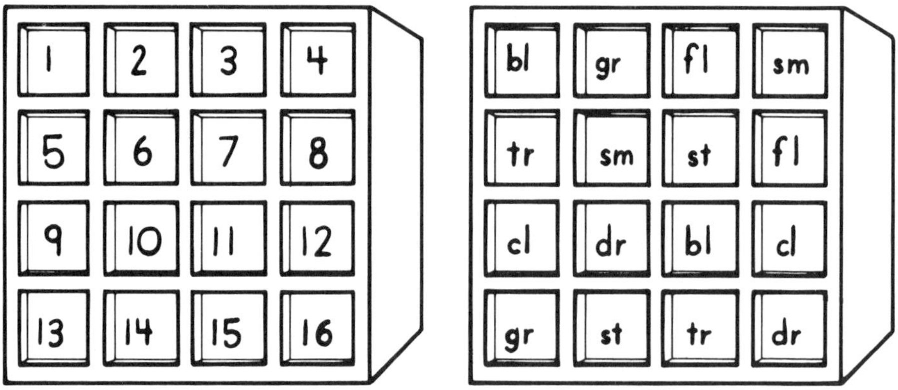

Consonant Scramble

Skill Development: Construction and identification of initial blend words.

Construction: On 3″ x 5″ cards, print consonant blend words with scrambled letters. Group all words containing the same blend. Put each group of scrambled words in a different envelope.

Utilization: Give an envelope to each player. The object of the game is to unscramble the words. The teacher calls time after ten minutes or less. A score of three points is given for each word that is unscrambled correctly. The players with the three highest scores read their words aloud to the group.

Scrambled Words

bl	**fr**	**st**	**cr**
labck	refe	mapst	meacr
tealbkn	denfri	tands	kecre
olbod	rifayd	rats	roscs
elub	tufir	tians	dowcr
slebs	zoerf	pets	rcy
dibln	ryf	pots	nowrc
nolbd	rofg	votes	koroc
moolb	notrf	sydut	proc
wolb	shefr	tays	rowc

gr	sl	tw	sk
wogr	dels	deewt	sikff
undrog	plees	ceitw	likls
morog	lieds	gitw	chetsk
tereg	pils	wirtl	disk
regen	lows	switt	misk
tearg	leavs	gantw	niks
ragy	laps	weett	ritks
pearg	ciels	leevwt	nukks
eardg	seypel	newtty	keats

Consonant Scrabble

Purpose: Develops the ability to spell consonant blend words.

Construction: Draw many squares on a large, heavy 20″ x 20″ board. Put numbers in the upper right-hand corner of each square. Take two colors of cubical wooden blocks and write an alphabet letter on each side of the blocks. Each player should use a different color.

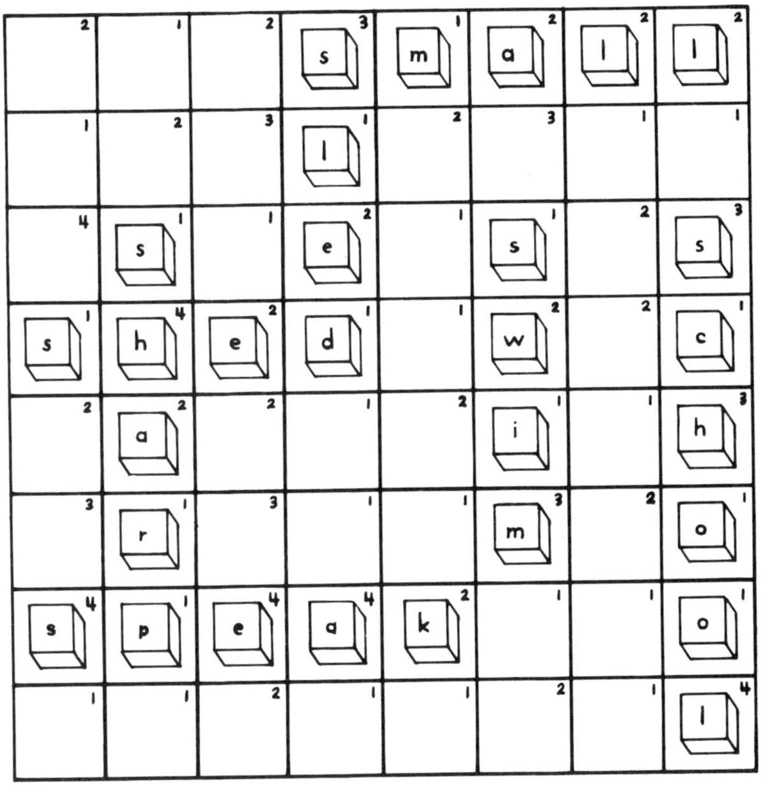

Utilization: Give each player ten blocks to start the game and additional blocks as needed so that he will always have ten blocks with which to form a word. A player scores points by placing the blocks in the squares to form words. Each word must begin with a consonant blend. The player whose word crosses another's word on the board gets an additional five points.

Ring-a-blend

Skill Development: Visual and auditory perception of initial consonant blends.

Construction: Use a piece of four-inch-thick styrofoam 30″ x 20″. Push nine large primary pencils (the kind that do not have erasers) into the styrofoam. Write blends on small cards and attach to the styrofoam near each pencil. The cards may be changed when practice is needed with other blends.

Utilization: From a distance of four to eight feet, a player tries to ring the pencils with plastic rings. (These plastic rings may be cut from plastic lids.) A player scores five points for ringing a pencil. He scores an extra five points if he can give a blend word for the blend represented by that pencil. Each player should get nine chances. The highest possible score is ninety. As many as five may play the game.

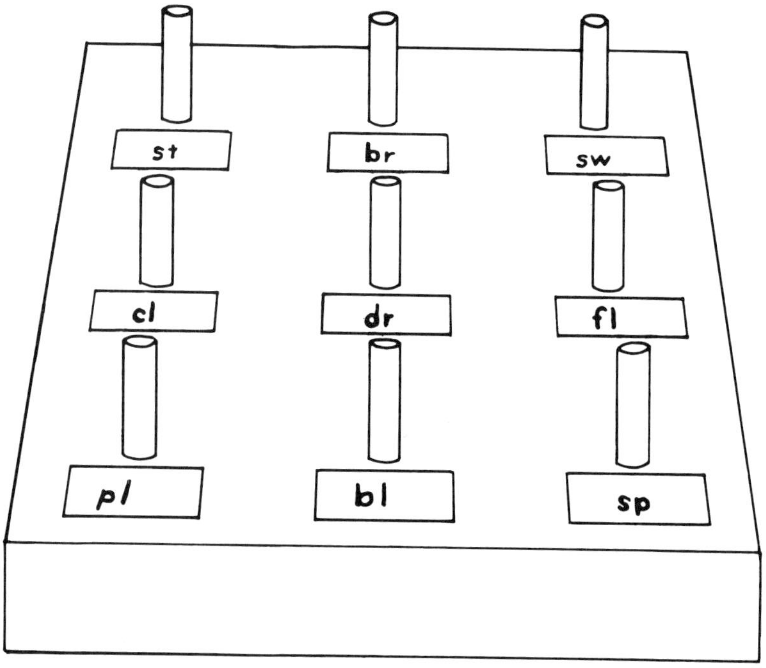

Final Blends Bingo

Skill Development: Visual and auditory perception of final consonant sounds.

Construction: Cut several cards 10″ x 6″. Divide the cards into twenty-five spaces by drawing four lines down each card 2½″ apart and four lines across 1½″ apart. Write the final sounds in twenty-four of the spaces, leaving the center space for a small picture. The sounds should be arranged in a different order on each card. Use these sounds:

ct	lk	ng	th	sp	pt
mp	ft	rt	lb	ld	ck
st	nk	lf	lp	nt	sh
ch	sk	nt	nd	lt	rl

Utilization: The teacher calls a list of words containing the final sounds. After a word is called, each student covers the appropriate final sound. For example, when the word *stamp* is called, the student covers *mp*. A straight row of correct responses wins the game.

ct	mp	st	ch	lk
ft	nk	sk	ng	rt
lf	nt		th	lb
lp	nd	sp	ld	nt
lt	pt	ck	sh	rl

Chapter 8

INDEPENDENT ACTIVITIES

These are ideas that may be used as self-directed activities. The pupil may be asked to keep records of the activities that he completed successfully. It is suggested that the teacher introduce a similar idea or skill in order to acquaint the student with the correct procedure. These ideas may be presented by:

1. Listing the directions on charts.
2. Duplicating or mimeographing directions for group seatwork.
3. Putting directions on acetate to use on the overhead projector for small group activities.
4. Recording directions on individual file cards, tagboard, or poster-board. Number each card or color code the cards to differentiate between categories or skills. The pupils are directed to choose a card from the file, take it to their seats, and follow the written directions.

Phonetic Analysis and Word Study

Part I—Pink Cards

1. Write a word that begins with each of these letters: *g, k, w, n, s, l, m, p, b, r.*
2. Use *p, r, c, m,* and *f,* to make new words from *an.*
3. Make word families from these: *ill, all, ound, ing, ake, et, ick, at, in.*
4. Look at these words: *fed, red, sun, fun.* Put the right word in each space below:

   a. Yesterday, we ________ our cat.
   b. Our flag is ________, white, and blue.
   c. Playing ball is ________.
   d. The ________ is very hot.

5. Write words that sound like these but are spelled differently:

hear	too	there	blue	know
see	rode	ate	deer	maid

6. Write a word that sounds like each one of these words:

best	shirt	sleep	pump
show	make	play	look
right	pocket	meet	fable

7. Write twenty words that begin with: *sh, ch, wh, th.*
8. Write a word that begins with each of these blends: *sl, gr, bl, st, br, cl, sm, dr, gl.*
9. Write twenty words with the short sound of *i.*
10. Write twenty words with long vowel sounds.
11. Write fifteen words with short vowel sounds.
12. Write two words that have each of these double vowels: *ea, ai, oa, oo, ee.*
13. Write an antonym for each of these words: *sour, white, work, small, old, long, first, strong, early.*
14. Write these letters. Put in the missing letters of the alphabet.

    a b c — e f g — i — k l — n o p — r — — u — w x — —

15. Rearrange these names in alphabetical order according to the last name:

Roy Valentine	Nancy Martino	Dan Price	Roy Dale
Tom Kent	Betty Adams	Linda Harris	John Zachary
Sue Jackson	John Roach	Tom Norton	Sam Fisher
Ted Grant	Jim Brown	Linda Cash	Maria Sanchez

16. Put these words in alphabetical order:

puzzle	space	bleed	village	candle
rocket	atmosphere	finish	stumble	queen
umpire	pumpkin	river	beautiful	olive

17. Underline the little word in each of these words:

letter	stand	wheat	parent	funny
catch	basket	ball	mitten	told

18. Underline the base word in these words:

safety	named	sweetly	sadness
washed	laughing	barked	tallest
softly	singing	noiseless	kinder

19. Copy words from your library book that have double letters and underline the letters. (Example: mi*dd*le, ha*pp*y)

20. Divide these words into syllables:

letter	signal	basket	friendly
summer	rabbit	orbit	funny
kitten	happen	today	stupid

21. Use the dictionary to define these words:

statue	steeple	stupid	stake	staple
sterilize	steward	stump	stunt	stoop

Creative Activities

Part I—Yellow Cards

1. Finish this story about yourself:

   My name is______________________________.
   I am________________years old.
   I like to________.
   My best friend is___________________________.
   When I grow up, I want to be_____________________.
2. Read this poem. Draw a picture illustrating the poem. (Any suitable poem may be used here.)
3. Paint a picture at the easel.
4. Draw a picture of a big, beautiful, blue bird.
5. Draw and color pictures of things that are round.
6. Draw a picture of something hard, something soft, something beautiful, and something ugly.
7. Draw a picture of what you would like to be when you grow up.
8. Draw a picture of your house and your family.
9. Choose five of these fruits to draw and color: apple, orange, grapes, pear, banana, grapefruit.
10. Draw a funny picture of one of these sentences:

    A boy has a bucket for a hat.
    A flower has arms and legs.
    A clock has big red ears.
11. Draw a picture of one of these helpers:

policeman	nurse	fireman	bus driver
mailman	teacher	dentist	librarian
doctor	milkman	lawyer	pilot

12. Draw a picture of yourself doing one of these:

Having fun in the park.	Going to school.
Shopping with mother.	Eating cotton candy.

13. Draw a picture illustrating the title of your library book.
14. Draw a picture showing what might have happened in your library book.
15. Find pictures of animals and paste them in your scrapbook.
16. Find pictures of things on the farm and paste them in your scrapbook.
17. Find pictures of things to wear and paste them in your scrapbook.
18. Write a letter to someone in the class and put it in the class mailbox.
19. Write your own poem.
20. Write sentences using the following words:

will	come	has	were	make
well	came	had	was	made

21. Choose five classmates and practice writing their names.
22. Write the months of the year and their abbreviations.

Phonetic Analysis and Word Study

Part II—Green Cards

1. In the word *cook,* you hear the hard *c* sound. In the word *race,* you hear the soft *c* sound. Write the words below. Tell if the *c* has a hard or a soft sound:

picture	cub	piece	count	princess
race	city	cage	corn	since

2. In the word *gum,* g has a hard sound. In the word *gem,* g has a soft sound. Write the words below. After each word write *h* if g is hard and *s* if the g is soft.

giant	gate	magic	gather	gallop
fog	snug	again	bag	dragon
sponge	hinge	strange	stage	fudge

3. Add *er* to the list of words below. Use the words in sentences.

fast	cold	new	warm	deep
soon	kind	bright	dark	fair
black	light	old	close	hard
clean	long	small	dear	near

4. If a word contains a short vowel sound and ends with a final consonant, the final consonant is often doubled before adding an ending, as *rub,* rubbed, rubbing. Add *ed* and *ing* to these words:

drop	clap	sod	wed	nap
trot	rot	plan	hug	dip
chop	rob	stop	bet	fan

5. Say these words: *helpful, restful.* The *ful* is called a suffix. The words to which suffixes are added are called root words. Add *ful* to these root words:

arm	color	delight	help	mouth	pain
bash	cup	truth	joy	power	thank

6. The vowel digraph *oo* may have the sound of *oo* as in *book* or the sound of *oo* as in *soon.* In the words below, circle *oo* as in *book.* Underline *oo* as in *soon.*

moon	brook	pool	balloon
zoo	rooster	took	shook
cookies	cool	choose	looked

7. Consonants that are not heard in a word are called silent consonants. Write these words. Draw a line through the consonants that are silent.

wrist	sign	half	sight	guess
fasten	knot	knob	wrap	fudge
thumb	palm	catch	rhyme	climb

8. In these words, the *t* is silent. Use these words in sentences. You may use the dictionary.

often	castle	fasten	thistle
Christmas	bustle	mortgage	soften

9. In these words, the *h* is silent. Use each word in a sentence. You may use your dictionary.

aghast	exhibit	laugh	whether
exhaust	rhubarb	flight	ghost

10. The *l* is silent in these words. Use each word in a sentence. You may use your dictionary.

calm	psalm	calf	talk
folk	chalk	half	walk

11. Write the words below. Put a triangle and a circle beside each word. Inside the triangle write the number of vowel letters. Inside the circle write the number of vowel sounds.

sport	stop	brave	nickname	seed
tiptop	classmate	weekday	rosebud	leader
barnyard	gift	pipe	third	learning

12. Write the following words. Beside each word write the number of syllables in the word.

blanket	afternoon	barbecue	reptile	memory
elephant	bulletin	earth	potato	subject
notebook	equator	against	inhuman	kindergarten

13. Write these words. Mark the vowel in the first syllable as long or short.

letter	victory	advertise	tomato	dynamo
runner	signal	super	handle	contain
bubble	republic	buffalo	abdomen	believe
elastic	teacher	alcohol	master	until

14. Write words with prefixes to match these definitions:

not sure____________________
money that comes in____________________
not happy____________________
to return money____________________
take the place of____________________
closed in on all sides____________________
to go back____________________

15. Match these words with the definitions below: dethrone, deform, confirm, degrade, contest, confine, conform, define, depress, condense.

to press down____________________
keep within limits____________________
reduce to a lower rank____________________
remove from a throne____________________
act according to rule____________________
to verify____________________
spoil the shape of____________________
make clear the meaning____________________
a competition____________________
make thicker or more compact____________________

16. Underline the word that fits each definition.

a. *not able*
undue
unable
uncommon

b. *put into words*
exhale
expose
express

c. *tell how to do*
explain
excite
exclaim

d. *reveal or deprive of shelter*
expose
expand
exist

17. Use the following words in sentences. You may use the dictionary.

humorous	perilous	nervous
vigorous	murderous	odorous
mountainous	marvelous	studious
joyous	mysterious	famous
courageous	prosperous	dangerous

Creative Activities

Part II—Orange Cards

1. Read a library book. Fill out a book report for your library book.
2. Draw the characters in your library book. Write a short paragraph about each character.
3. Write your own story about one of the pictures in your library book.
4. Write another ending for your library story.
5. Imagine that you could change things the way you'd like them.

   What things would you change?
   What would you make sweeter?
   What would you make smaller?
   What would you give wings?
   What would you make heavier?
   What would you make larger?
   What would you make faster?
   What would you make longer?
6. Use your imagination. What might happen if these things were changed?

   If elephants were the size of cocker spaniels?
   If dogs had wings?
   If everyone's hair turned green overnight?
7. Have you ever heard the expressions "sharp as a tack" or "fit as a fiddle"? Fill in these blanks. Try to be original.

   funny as ____________
   hard as ____________
   crooked as ____________
   wet as ____________
   as cool as ____________
   like mixing ____________
   sells like ____________
   nervous as ____________
   like finding ____________
   as smart as ____________
8. When you see a peacock or read about one, the idea of feathers, beauty, or color may come to your mind. What ideas come to your mind when you think of these things?

   soul music
   milk
   tennis shoes
   a bicycle
   a large shady tree
   a strawberry
   a honeybee
   a tall mountain
   a creek
9. Write the words below. In each row, circle the word that does not belong.

a. elm	maple	colonial	spruce
b. Atlanta	Colorado	Detroit	Boston
c. Miami	Kentucky	New York	Georgia

d. apple	rose	gardenia	carnation
e. boy	skirt	blouse	dress
f. hammer	saw	car	wrench
g. banana	bean	apple	orange
h. corn	cabbage	pear	lettuce

10. Look at the picture on the left of the card. Write a story about the picture. Give your story a title.
11. Look at the picture. What kind of store is this? Describe what you see in the window.
12. Tell a story about this picture. Give your story a title. Has this ever happened to you?
13. Choose picture number 1 or number 2. What would you do if this happened to you?
14. What would you get if you could buy ten items?
15. Where would you go if you could take a trip anywhere? Why would you go?
16. Would you go on a camping trip or on a trip to the moon? Why? What would you do?
17. What would you do if you were lost in the woods?
18. Before you read a library book, write the story the title makes you think of. Then after you have read the book, write a report of the real story.
19. Write a letter of appreciation to an author you admire, asking him questions and telling him what you thought of his story. Send him a story of yours on the same subject as his.
20. Make a list of things that you want to know more about.

Chapter 9

VOCABULARY EXTENSION AND COMPREHENSION

A reading program is incomplete if word attack skills are taught in isolation. If and when this occurs, the reader perhaps learns to decode the printed symbols, but comprehension is not taking place. Thus, it is impossible to separate vocabulary or word meaning and comprehension. Word meanings, important as they are in developing all levels of comprehension—concrete, abstract, and creative—need to be supported by further learnings.

Concrete thinking, which concerns itself primarily with getting the facts or details from the printed page, is frequently the only kind of comprehension exercises that are required of the students. There is no depth in this kind of thinking. It is at the lowest level in the hierarchy of thought-getting skills; yet it is the one on which many basal readers expend their efforts. The school systems are changing, but there are still many districts where monies may only be spent for basal texts as the major source of educating children.

Abstract comprehension is at the next level in the hierarchy of thinking skills because it requires the learner to perform many different tasks. He must supply information by adding to what is factual. He must be adept at evaluating and interpreting ideas and opinions. Most of all, he must be capable of predicting outcomes and summarizing information.

Creative comprehension is at the highest level in the hierarchy of thinking skills. It is at this level that the learner reads the printed page but ventures beyond the author's point of view. He attempts to seek out and express his own ideas and opinions. Unlike the other areas of comprehension, creative comprehension has no specific or correct answers. Hence, the learner questions, inquires, and is driven forward with intense motivation and urgency.

It is the purpose of this chapter to provide the teacher with exercises and suggestions that help to extend vocabulary and comprehension skills.

My Word Folder

Purpose: Helps child organize and keep a record of words he does and doesn't know.

Construction: Cut a piece of posterboard 22″ x 10″ in size. Fold the bottom up three inches to make a pocket and fold the board in half. Using colored tape, tape the pockets on both sides and all the way around to add color. Ask each student to put his favorite picture on the front of his folder.

Utilization: Let the student write words that he wishes to learn on cards and keep them in his folder. When he can pronounce, spell, and define the word, he may place it in the pocket on the left side. This is a good way to review missed spelling words.

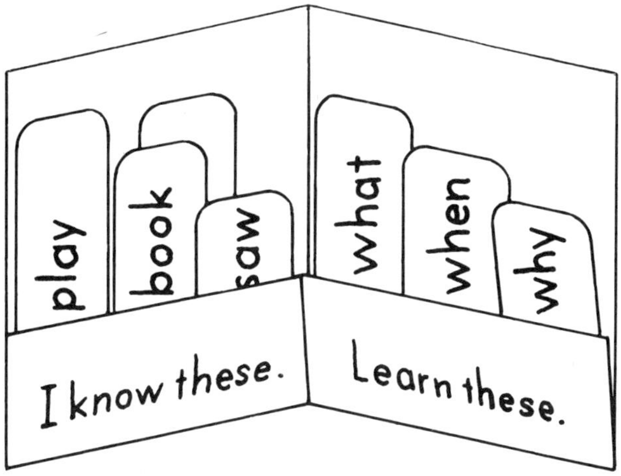

Dial-a-poem

Purpose: To develop an interest in and a fondness for poetry.

Construction: Draw the outline of a clock with a face seventeen inches in diameter. Make a base for the clock twenty inches wide. The height of the clock from top to bottom is twenty-four inches. Paste pictures instead of numbers around the face of the clock. Attach a hand with a paper fastener. Cut a duplicate shape of the entire base of the clock. Staple or tape this duplicate behind the original base of the clock, leaving the top part open to form a pocket to hold poems written on 7″ x 11″ cards.

Utilization: First, a student turns the dial to a picture. Then he reads the poem that goes with the picture. The teacher should read the poems to immature readers or have an able student do the reading. The poems may also be used for choral reading and to inspire creative art expressions.

*The Little Turtle**

There was a little turtle.
He lived in a box.
He swam in a puddle.
He climbed on a rock.

He snapped at a mosquito.
He snapped at a flea.
He snapped at a minnow.
And he snapped at me.

He caught the mosquito.
He caught the flea.
He caught the minnow.
But he didn't catch me.

Vachel Lindsay

*From *Collected Poems,* by Vachel Lindsay. Copyright 1920 by The Macmillan Company, renewed 1948 by Elizabeth C. Lindsay. Reprinted by permission.

Big Book

Purpose: This large book may be used for experience stories, creative writing, initial sounds, field trip experiences, class pictures, or any other activity.

Construction: Using a large piece of cardboard, make an 18″ x 25″ book cover. Cover this cardboard with cloth. Stitch in large sheets of newsprint for the pages (use large needle and thread). After the pages are stitched in, paste the first sheet of the newsprint to the cardboard cover. Paste the last page of the newsprint to the inside back of the covered cardboard.

Utilization: Have the students type or write their own stories to be mounted in this large book. A book may be made twice the size of this one so that it can stand on the floor.

Read! Do What It Says

Skill Development: Following simple directions.

Construction: Cut manila folders in half. Copy simple phrases and sentences giving instructions from the basal reader text. Write each of these directions on a folder "card." Put these large cards into another folder.

Utilization: The student takes a card to his seat, reads the directions, and follows them.

Reusable Worksheets

Purpose: Diagnosis or evaluation of any reading skill.

Construction: Mount a worksheet on tagboard. Cover with transparent plastic and tape all sides. Keep these worksheets in a skills file.

Utilization: Ask the pupils to use a grease pencil when doing the worksheets. The plastic may be rubbed clean and used again. Be sure to put the directions for the worksheet on the back if they are not included in the printed lesson.

Football Is My Game

Purpose: Improve phrase reading by capitalizing on the interest of the student. Aids in oral language expression.

Construction: Draw and cut out a football 12″ long. Attach a pocket cut in the same shape. Insert phrase cards that the student has prepared.

Utilization: Some of the phrases such as "field goal," "off sides," and "first down" may be read and explained or discussed by the student. The teacher may wish to have the student use the phrase in a complete sentence.

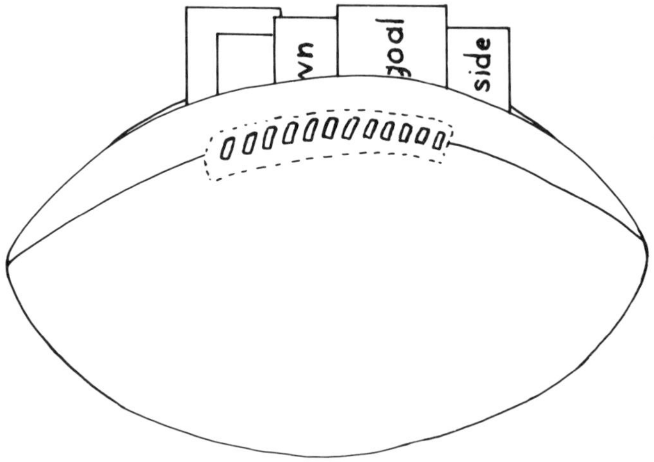

Months of the Year

Skill Development: Students learn to pronounce and spell the months of the year, become familiar with the history of each month, and learn the important holidays in each month.

Construction: On a 28″ x 22″ heavy board or bulletin board, place twelve pockets made from tag, corrugated paper, or felt. On the outside of each pocket write the number of the month. Include on cards in each pocket the following items for that month:

1. The name of the month.
2. The abbreviation for that month, if there is one.
3. The name of the month divided into syllables.

4. Holidays in the month.
5. Birthdays of important people.
6. A small calendar for that month.
7. The history or origin of the name of that month.
8. Birthdays of classmates.
9. Scrambled letters for the name of that month.
10. Questions about that particular month.

Utilization: The student removes the contents of a pocket; for example, the pocket numbered 2, which would be February. The teacher asks the child to do the following things:

1. Match the abbreviation of the month with the name.
2. Put the syllables together to form the name of the month.
3. Use the small calendar to circle all important holidays and birthdays.
4. Write the names of classmates on the calendar on the dates of their birthdays.
5. Put the scrambled letters in the correct order.
6. Answer these questions:
   a. The third Tuesday falls on what date?
   b. How many Sundays are there in the month?
   c. The 15th falls on what day?
   d. The first Sunday falls on what date?
   e. The last Saturday comes on what date?

Scrambles

Skill Development: Classification skills.

Construction: On 3″ x 5″ cards, write scrambled words for *art, music, sports,* and *mathematics.* Put each group of words in a long white envelope. Keep all of the envelopes in a folder when not in use. Write the directions on the storage folders. Include a corrected teacher's copy.

Utilization: The student is to unscramble the words in the envelope. For example, when unscrambled the letters *seale* from the art envelope would spell *easel.* To make the game interesting, set a time limit of ten minutes. When time is up, give each student five points for each correct word.

Synonyms, Antonyms, and Homonyms

Skill Development: Gives practice with words that have the same or nearly the same meaning, with words that are opposite in meaning, and with words that sound alike but are spelled differently and have different meanings.

Construction: Draw twenty-five squares on 7″ x 7″ cards. Write a word in each square. No two cards should have the same arrangement of words. Write the antonym, synonym, or homonym for each word on cards the size of a square.

Utilization: The student covers the word on the card with the corresponding word. For example, the word *last* on the large card would be covered with the small card *first*.

day	old	last	up	in
boy	wet	stop	hard	no
walk	love	big	true	his
early	king	work	open	man
east	wife	long	cry	sit

Synonym Chart

Skill Development: Word meaning and comprehension.

Construction: Use pastel bristol board, 10″ x 22″. On each chart put a picture clue and words that describe the picture. For example, put a picture of a toy on a chart and the words *play, frolic, romp, amusement, enjoyment.* At the primary level, the teacher will have to prepare the chart. At the intermediate and upper levels, pupils may wish to prepare their own charts.

Utilization: The chart may be displayed on the bulletin board or somewhere in the classroom for reference.

Circus Words

Skill Development: Classifying words and phrases.

Construction: Draw and cut out an outline of a circus tent. Attach a pocket labeled "Circus Words" before drawing lines and adding fringes. Insert words about the circus on small cards. Make a flag and attach it to the top of the tent.

Utilization: Ask students to take a word from the pocket, pronounce it, and use it in a sentence.

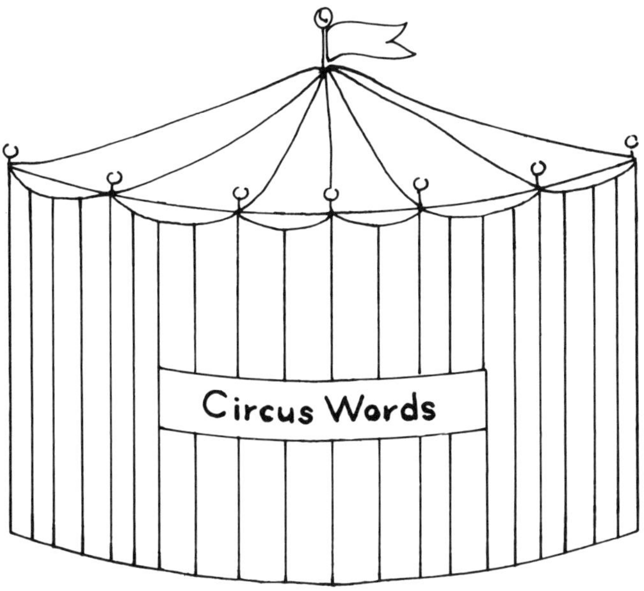

Wise Old Owl

Skill Development: Independent reading.

Construction: Draw and cut out a picture of an owl. Attach a pocket in the middle of the owl's body.

Utilization: Each student fills out a card on which he records his name and the titles of the books that he has read. The student may enter the name of the book after he is able to discuss, summarize, or illustrate it. The owl may be attached to a bulletin board. If so, make a construction paper branch for the owl to perch on. Mount other pockets to hold student cards on the bulletin board. The five students who have the highest number of recorded books may place them in the owl pocket.

My Own Dictionary

Skill Development: Word meaning and alphabetical sequence.

Construction: Make a dictionary using construction paper or newsprint for the pages. Make the cover from felt, posterboard, wallpaper, or cardboard covered with cloth. Bind the book with loose-leaf rings, paper fasteners, or staples. At the top of each page, write a letter of the alphabet or attach a picture representing a letter.

Utilization: Each student should keep a file of unfamiliar words on 3″ x 5″ cards. The unfamiliar word should be written at the top of the card with the meaning under the word. At the end of the unit or grading period, the student lists the words in his dictionary in alphabetical order. The repetition of rewriting each word will help the student with vocabulary development.

A Reading Record

Skill Development: Independent reading.

Construction: Make several pockets in the shape of a boxcar by folding 12″ x 8″ pieces of cardboard in half. Tape each side, leaving the top open to form a pocket. Insert a card for each pupil in these pockets. Draw, cut out, and attach the other parts of the train.

Utilization: When a pupil has read a book and can describe or tell something about the book, he may record the title of the book on his card. Keep this record on an attractive bulletin board.

Signs You Should Know

Purpose: Aids in the ability to read important signs.

Construction: Cut out a large octagon-shaped stop sign from red showboard. Cut three sides of another octagon the same size and attach it to the bottom half of the whole stop sign to form a pocket. Use white cloth tape to hold the pocket in place. Use the same white tape to complete the border around the sign. Write all words and phrases in capital letters on cards. Insert these words and phrases in the pocket.

1. YIELD RIGHT-OF-WAY
2. DEAD END
3. RAILROAD CROSSING
4. STOP
5. DO NOT ENTER
6. DYNAMITE
7. SCHOOL ZONE
8. EXIT
9. DANGER
10. BEWARE OF DOG

Utilization: Ask a student to read the signs, tell where he might see the signs, and explain what each one means.

Compound Words

Skill Development: Recognition and classification of compound words.

Construction: Use 9″ x 20″ fourteen-ply showboard to make this compound word chart. Classify the words under various headings. For example, under the heading of *people,* these words would be listed: classmate, cowboy, foreman, grandfather, milkman, and newsboy. Other headings may be *places, rides, times, things.*

Utilization: The teacher initiates the following activity with the class before the chart is prepared: Ask the pupils what a compound word is. Several definitions may be suggested before the correct one is given. Place five headings on the chalkboard: places, people, rides, things, and times. Ask the children for compound words that will fit under each heading. Transfer the written material from the board to the charts. Leave ample space so that additional words may be added.

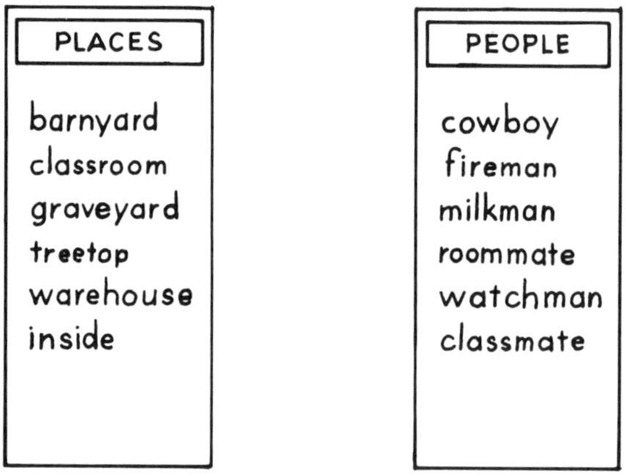

Alphabetizing House

Skill Development: Alphabetizing words.

Construction: Make an outline of your favorite house on fourteen-ply showboard. Staple on felt windows, leaving the top part open to form pockets. Place a number of words written on individual cards in each pocket. Cut an outline of a door from white tagboard and paste it to the house.

Utilization: A group of six students may work with the alphabetizing house at one time. Each student chooses a pocket of words to alphabetize. They may correct each other's work and choose another pocket until each pupil has worked with all of the words. For evaluation purposes, the teacher may wish to stop the group at a given point and check the words in the pockets. In this way, the teacher will be able to determine which student is having difficulty with the skill.

Er, Ir, Ur

Skill Development: Pronunciation and spelling.

Construction: On a 14″ x 20″ piece of matboard, mount a white fence, a red barn, and a brown rooster atop the fence. Make a large pocket that can be divided into three compartments to hold the word cards of *er, ir*, and *ur* words.

Utilization: After the introduction of the skill, the students may use the word cards for pronunciation, spelling, or practicing dictionary skills.

Scrambled Contractions

Skill Development: Usage of contractions.

Construction: Cut posterboard into small strips 11″ x 1″. Tape these strips across an 11″ x 14″ piece of posterboard to form slots. Attach library card pockets on the back to hold words.

Utilization: Remove words from the pocket on the back. Place contractions in the slots on the left and the words they are composed of on the right. The children should rearrange the contractions to match and then use each in a sentence.

Garbled Sentences

Skill Development: Sequential development—arranging words and phrases into sentences.

Construction: Using black posterboard, construct a 15″ x 22″ outline of a traffic light. Cut three circles—red, yellow, and green—about five inches in diameter. Cut three half circles of the same three colors and attach each to the circle of the same color by stapling it around the bottom. Make three sets of small cards—red, yellow, and green. Write the following words or phrases on each card:

red cards: Canaries, Parents, Children, Teachers, Old people, Many criminals, Puppies, Some kittens, People, Some fathers
yellow cards: are sometimes sad, are happiest, play games, like to swim, are unhappy, are disappointed, are put in prison, are adorable, are cuddly, are delightful

green cards: when their children move away, during the summer, when pupils obey, to avoid being bored, when they break the law, and have soft brown eyes, and sometimes very playful, when they chirp and sing, when they live alone, when the new baby is a boy

Utilization: Explain to the children that these groups of words and phrases were once sentences. They have been divided into three parts and each part placed in a different pocket. Ask them to see if they can put together at least five good sentences by using a card from each of the three pockets for each sentence. Have them read the sentences aloud. Later, they may make up words and phrases of their own for use in the pockets.

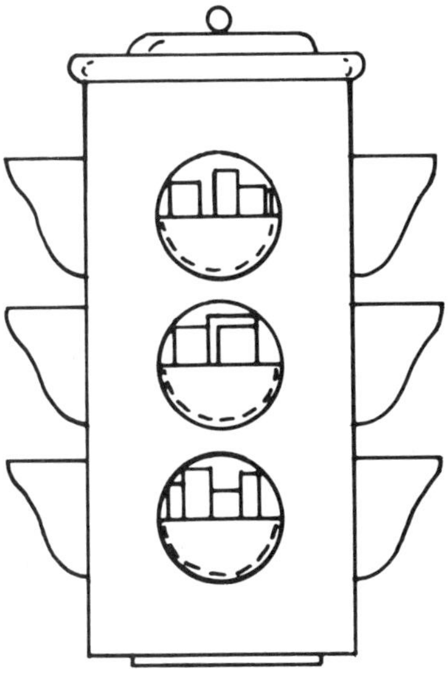

Funny Expressions

Skill Development: Practice with reading and figurative language.

Construction: Cut an eighteen-inch circle from green posterboard. Cut a partial circle and staple it around the bottom edges of the circle to form a pocket. Make a large smiling face by attaching eyes, nose, and a mouth. Write these sentences on cards and insert them in the pocket. The words shown in italics here should be underlined on your cards.

1. Don't *throw your money away* at the circus.
2. Father *flew down* the stairs.
3. *Night fell* as we approached the harbor.
4. He *made his mark* as a successful businessman.
5. Mother *lost her temper* and threw the dish on the floor.

Utilization: Have the students read each sentence and explain the meaning of the underlined words. Ask the children to make up their own sentences using the underlined words or to make up original sentences.

I Like Baseball

Skill Development: Phrase reading and oral language expression.

Construction: Use 18″ x 12″ posterboard. Attach an 18″ x 5″ pocket to hold word and phrase cards. Add picture clues to the top part of the board.

Utilization: Ask a pupil to make a collection about his favorite sport or hobby. Help the child collect appropriate words and phrases to be written on cards and placed in the pocket. The children are to read, discuss, and explain each group of words.

Word Meanings

Skill Development: Comprehension of words and sentences.

Construction: Cut strips of manila tag 18″ x 3″. Write completion sentences on the strips. Write three possible answers at the end of the sentence.

Utilization: The student uses a paper clip to indicate the correct answer. He may read the sentences aloud to the teacher after he has completed the exercise.

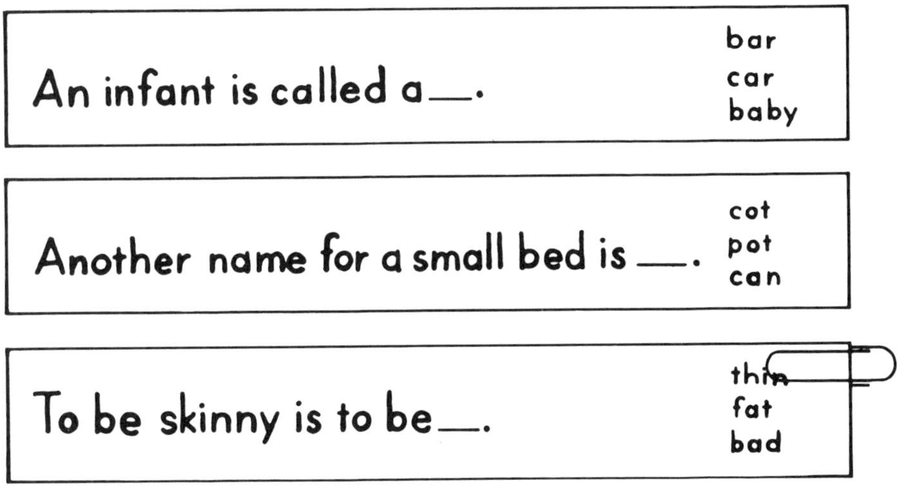

Reading the Newspaper

Skill Development: Skimming to get the main idea, reading to obtain factual information, and reading for enjoyment.

Construction: Glue together several sheets of newsprint and tape the outer edges. Cut a pocket in the lower portion. (The project may also be made from posterboard.) Cut articles on sports and current events, comic strips, and headlines from the local newspaper and mount them on tagboard or bristol board cards. Write discussion questions on the back of each card. Insert the cards in the pocket.

Utilization: The children are to choose one or more cards from the pocket and either write or discuss the answers to the questions listed on the back of each card. For example, an article about a baseball game may have these questions listed on the back: (1) Define these terms: inning, single, sacrifice fly, error, balk. (2) Which team won the game? (3) Who were the outstanding players in the game?

Multiple Meanings

Skill Development: Word meanings.

Construction: Cut ten pieces of 12″ x 22″ bristol board and attach them with two loose-leaf rings. Paste a picture at the top of each page and write descriptive words under each picture. For example, these words could be written under the picture of an apple: *delectable, savory, appetizing, juicy, crisp.*

Utilization: Have the children pronounce each word under a picture and look up the word in the dictionary, noting the diacritical markings. Let each child select and mount a picture and write a list of descriptive words for his picture.

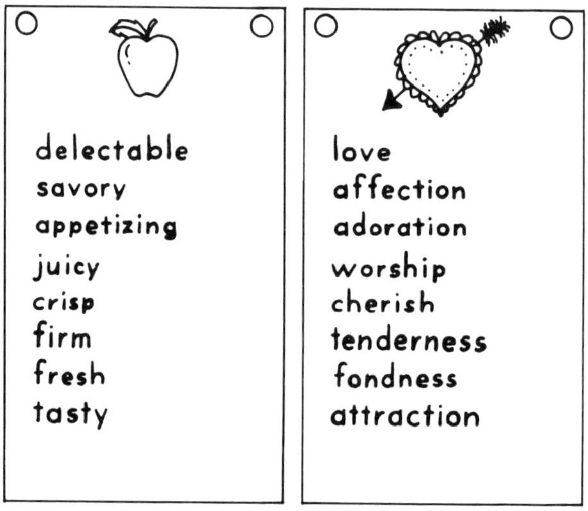

Parts of a Book

Purpose: To explain the purpose of different parts of a book.

Construction: Draw two outlines of a book on bristol board and staple the two together to form a pocket. Leave the top or the right side open to hold cards. Write the following definitions on one end of 10″ x 4″ strips of tagboard and mount a library card pocket at the other end.

1. Lists the title of the book, the author, the illustrator, and the publisher.
2. Gives an overview of the book. Points out the importance and purpose of the book. May also include an acknowledgment.
3. Lists all topics, subjects, and people discussed or mentioned in a book and gives a page number where each may be found.
4. Includes materials that are not an essential part of the text but that are helpful to the reader, such as word lists, charts, tables, and explanations that are too long for footnoting.
5. Provides the setting for the chapters that are to follow. Comes after the table of contents.
6. Lists part and chapter titles and page numbers.
7. An alphabetical listing of all related reference materials—books, magazines, and audiovisuals.
8. An alphabetical listing of all words and their definitions that are necessary to understanding the content of the book.

On 1″ x 3″ cards write the answer to each of the definitions and put the cards in the book pocket along with the definition cards. The answers are: 1. Title page, 2. Preface, 3. Index, 4. Appendix, 5. Introduction, 6. Table of contents, 7. Bibliography, 8. Glossary.

Utilization: Ask the students to read each definition and to match it with the correct answer card. The answer card should be inserted into the library card pocket on the end of the definition strip.

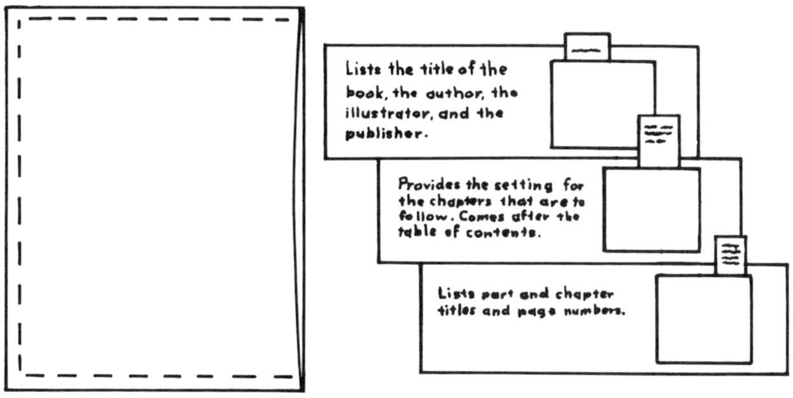

Similes

Skill Development: Practice in figurative language.

Construction: Construct a matching board by attaching library card pockets to a piece of 18″ x 12″ showboard. The pockets should be placed in two equal vertical rows. Write incomplete phrases on cards of one color and the words that complete the phrases on cards of another color. Here are some sample phrases and words:

phrases	**words**
sweet as	honey
easy as	pie
sharp as a	tack
happy as a	lark
white as	snow
slow as a	snail
quick as a	wink
hard as	nails
smooth as	silk

Utilization: Explain to the children what similes are and how they are used in everyday language. Have the children complete each phrase by putting a phrase in the left pocket and the correct word in the right pocket. Ask the children to explain the literal meaning of each expression and allow them to make up their own similes.

Taking Advice

Skill Development: Comprehension and interpreting implied ideas.

Construction: On a piece of 18″ x 12″ showboard, mount a picture of a child doing one of the following or something similar: brushing his teeth, eating dinner, walking home from school, helping with chores around the house, or talking with someone on the street. Attach an 18″ x 3″ felt pocket to hold these sentences that have been written on 2″ x 12″ cards:

1. Brush your teeth after each meal and before you go to bed.
2. Eat the vegetables on your plate.
3. Always come home immediately after school or call your parents if you plan to visit friends.
4. Do your chores around the house early Saturday morning.
5. Don't stop to talk with strangers.
6. Never ride your bicycle across a busy street.

7. Always cover your mouth when coughing or sneezing.
8. Always be polite and courteous to others.

Utilization: The student should remove the cards from the pocket, read each carefully, and choose five as his assignment. Ask him these questions:

1. If your parents gave you this advice, how would you feel about it?
2. Who do you think would tell you to do these things?
3. Write your ideas and opinions on paper and prepare to discuss them with the class.

The United States

Purpose: To stimulate interest in reading and remembering factual information about various states.

Construction: Mount seven red stripes 1½″ wide on a 28″ x 22″ piece of white showboard. On the left side, mount a royal blue field 16″ x 11″. Cut out three white stars, print the name of a state on each, and mount them on the blue field. Write statements about the states on several other stars.

Utilization: Have the students read about the three states and then have them match the correct statement with each state by placing the star over the state star.

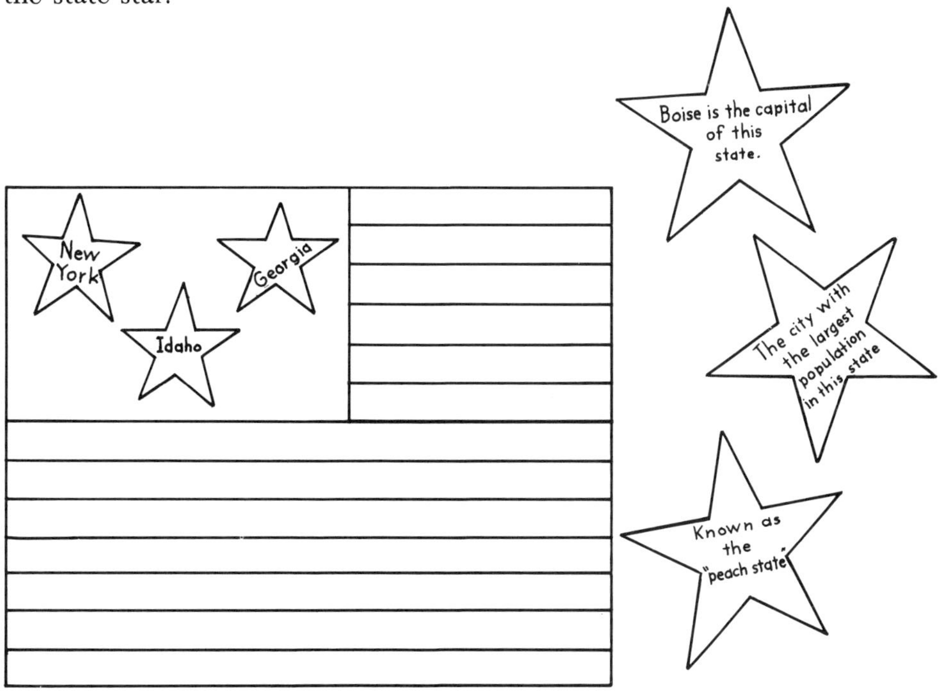

Transportation

Skill Development: Use of reference materials.

Construction: On posterboard draw and cut out an outline of a truck 24″ long and 12″ high. Cut another piece of posterboard the size of the trailer portion of the truck and staple it to the back of the truck, leaving the top open to form a pocket. Write these directions on cards and insert them in the pocket:

1. List at least ten means of transportation. Choose one for further study. Use the encyclopedia and other reference books to locate information.
2. Use the encyclopedia to find out what makes an airplane stay in the air. Prepare a report to present to the class. Be creative when presenting it—for example, use drawings, pictures, slides, or transparencies.
3. Who was Henry Ford? Use the library to find out more about him. Write a short biography about him and present it to the class.
4. Write a story about a trip you took away from home. Tell where you went, what happened on your trip, and what means of transportation you used.
5. Make a scrapbook about your favorite means of transportation. Some picture sources are: magazines, book jackets, postcards, travel bureau, chamber of commerce, original drawings.
6. Preview films, filmstrips, or slides on transportation. Choose one to share with the class. Make up some questions to ask after the presentation.

Utilization: Have a child select a card from the pocket on the truck and follow the directions on that card.

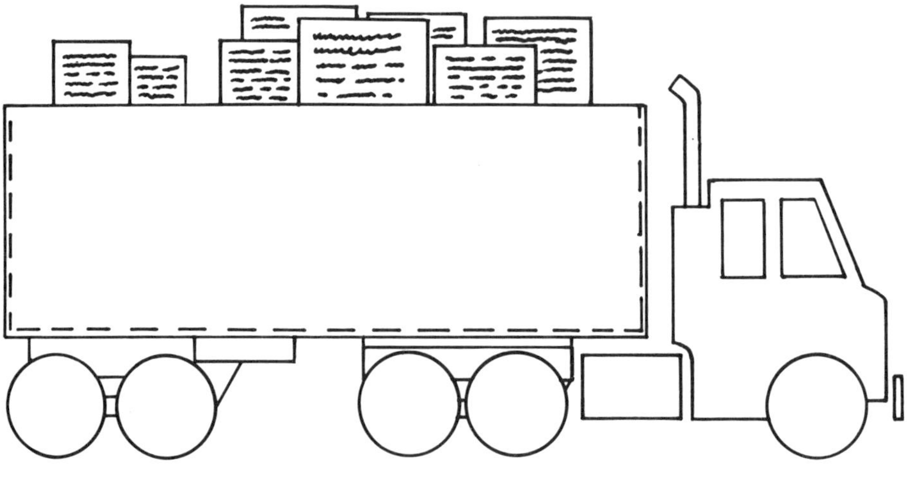

Chapter 10

ORAL LANGUAGE DEVELOPMENT

Oral language development is a vital part of the total school curriculum. One of the most important functions of the elementary teacher is to plan and execute programs that are sensitive to the language needs of each individual within the group. In reference to language development, most educators would agree that we must hear a word before we speak it, we must speak it before we read it, and we usually read it before we write it. Therefore, listening and speaking skills are a prerequisite to reading and writing skills.

The major goal of any oral language program should be to develop a smooth flow of ideas and thoughts. The teacher can be assured of a successful program if she motivates and encourages the child to talk, supplies interesting topics for the child to talk about, and gives him the opportunity to talk.

Among the varying language patterns that will be found in the average classroom, the following patterns should be closely observed by the teacher: (a) the pupil who seldom speaks except when answering with one word, (b) the pupil who talks so much that his classmates seldom get a chance to speak, (c) the shy and nervous student who speaks in a high-pitched voice, (d) the pupil who has severe speech defects and needs the assistance of a trained therapist, and (e) the student whose vocabulary is so broad and extensive that he expresses opinions and ideas clearly and distinctly.

The teachers should always keep in mind the importance of accepting the child's language. This language is a part of him and to reject it is to reject the child himself.

Let's Go Shopping

Construct a shopping bag from the lower portion of a grocery bag. Attach handles and paste pictures of vegetables and other foods cut from old magazines on the sides. Let the children find pictures of other foods and put them in the shopping bag. Have each child tell the class what he bought at the store.

Play House

Construct a small house from a box. Direct the child to cut pictures of furniture from old magazines. Let him name each piece of furniture and the room of the house where it belongs.

If constructing a house is not feasible, draw a large skeleton picture of a house on brown kraft paper. The picture should be drawn so that each room in the house shows: the living room, the dining room, the bedrooms, the kitchen, and the carport or garage. Let the children cut out pictures of furniture and paste them in the appropriate rooms. A small group of students can work on a project and later tell the rest of the class about it.

Descriptive Word Game

The teacher holds up a familiar object in order to elicit descriptive words such as *round, heavy, square,* etc. The object is shown and the teacher asks, "What is this?" "What shape is it?" The same procedure can be used to teach words like *thin, thick, above, below,* etc.

To illustrate abstract words like *off,* pictures may be used instead of objects. For example, the teacher shows a picture of a man's hat being blown off. The teacher asks, "What do you think blew his hat off?" Words must be pronounced clearly and distinctly so children learn differences between words like *off* and *of.*

Grocery Store

Use cardboard boxes to construct a grocery store. Empty cartons and small boxes can represent items that will be purchased. One child pretends he's the clerk in the store. The other children pretend to be shoppers. With older children, this helps to make mathematics a meaningful experience.

Riddles

The teacher asks a riddle:

I run down the street.
I bounce and jump and wag my tail.
I love to chase balls and cats.
When I'm happy, I bark.
I am a ______________________________.

Later, the children can make up riddles themselves. The child who guesses the riddle gets a chance to ask the next one.

What I Can Do Time

Have each child get up and tell the group about something that he can do. For example, I can wash dishes. I can hop like a rabbit. I can sing a song.

Field Trips

Discuss field trip experiences in small groups or as a whole group activity. Prepare questions that will evoke both factual and inferential answers from the children.

Show and Tell

Encourage the children to bring toys, souvenirs, collections, or other prize possessions to class. Call on a child to show some object and then tell all he can about it. Evaluate by asking what the children enjoyed most.

Interpreting Pictures

Show a picture to a group and have the children discuss either the main idea, the figures in the foreground or background, or the colors. Occasionally, specific questions may be asked, such as "What is the little boy holding in his hand?" "Where do you think he is going?" etc. Some children may be able to make up a short story of two or three sentences about the picture while the others listen for sequence of ideas.

Tape Recorder

Listen to and record the children's speech at the beginning of the school year. Note total number of words spoken, number of different words spoken, length of sentences used, the interest revealed, and consonant sounds mispronounced. Let the pupils compare progress in speech development at intervals during the school year.

Dictation

Children always enjoy dictating a letter to the parents who went with them to the zoo, to the firemen who showed them around the fire station, or to the child who is in the hospital.

Watching Game for Sequence

The teacher or a child performs a short series of acts, such as tapping on the desk, lifting a book, and then picking up a piece of chalk. The children are called upon to tell the nature and order of the act performed.

Rhyming from Pictures

On the chalkboard, the teacher places pictures of objects that rhyme, such as a picture of an apple, a pie, a hand, etc. The teacher points to the first picture and asks what it is. "Yes, it is a pie. Who can find another picture that rhymes with it?" This game may be varied by simply showing a picture and having the children give all the rhyming words they can.

Newsletter

The children discuss the important activities that have happened in the class during the week. The teacher records the information on the board. A newsletter is sent home to the parents to keep them informed of classroom activities. Friday is always an excellent day to send home such a letter.

Original Word-by-word Stories

The children sit in a circle. The teacher or a child starts off with a word such as "Oscar." The next child adds another and repeats the first, as "Oscar was." Each child adds a new word until a sentence is complete. The game can be continued along this general theme until a story about the initial word is complete. For a very immature group, it may be advisable to give practice in single sentences before continuity in theme is stressed.

Words That Describe

Find a large, colorful picture of a dog, cat, horse, man, baby, or any other expressive picture and mount it on the bulletin board, posterboard, or flannel board. Ask the children to give you words that describe the picture, such as *pretty, big, tall, lazy,* etc.

Supplying Endings

Read three or four lines of an unfamiliar story to the children and have them supply the ending. The story may be original or one that the teacher will read at a later time. For example, the teacher reads, "Nicky was a very sleepy little bear. He usually fell asleep while the other bears were all having fun. One day, Nicky fell asleep under a large oak tree. Suddenly he awoke with a start. Close by stood . . . "

Telephoning

The child uses the telephone in imaginative play. He calls home to see about lunch money or after-school plans. He uses the phone for ordering groceries and other supplies or for receiving and sending messages. The teacher should help the children increase their conversational ability and improve their enunciation in telephone conversations.

Guessing-rhyming Game

Say, "We are going to play a new guessing game today. This little boy is Bill." The teacher points to a picture or to a child whose name is Bill. "He lives on a big, high ________. Who can tell where Bill lives? It is a word that sounds like Bill. Yes, it is *hill.* Bill likes to sit on the window ________. Yes, *sill.* Who can give me another word that sounds like *Bill* and *sill?*"

Planning Activities

Give the children the opportunity to plan and prepare for trips and excursions. Have them talk about the benefits gained from the trips, discuss the work of the members of the class, and evaluate the trip.

Carrying Out Directions

The teacher and children play a direction game. Call a child to the front of the room and give him three simple directions to carry out. For example, say, "Go to the back of the room, touch the easel, then hop back to your seat." The children in the group note the accuracy of his response. Vary the tasks and make them interesting and amusing enough so that there is attentive listening as well as genuine enjoyment. Later, the number of assigned tasks may be increased.

Dramatization

Read a story and encourage the children to dramatize it. Still another way to encourage activity is for the group as a whole to supply lines in a familiar story. The teacher reads the story and the children take the part of such characters as Little Red Riding Hood or the Little Red Hen and the other animals.

Group Discussions

Encourage the children to talk about their vacations, experiences over the weekend, trips made with parents, interesting incidents and activities, a new baby in the family, etc. Evaluation by the group may follow if the teacher wishes to check attentiveness or memory for ideas.

BIBLIOGRAPHY

BARBE, WALTER B. *Educators' Guide to Personalized Reading Instruction.* Englewood Cliffs, N.J.: Prentice-Hall, Inc., 1961.

BOND, GUY L., and TINKER, MILES A. *Reading Difficulties: Their Diagnosis and Correction.* New York: Appleton-Century-Crofts, 1957.

CHALL, JEANNE. *Learning to Read: The Great Debate.* New York: McGraw-Hill, Inc., 1967.

DECHANT, EMERALD V. *Improving the Teaching of Reading.* Englewood Cliffs, N.J.: Prentice-Hall, Inc., 1964.

DELLA-PIANA, GABRILL M. *Reading Diagnosis and Prescription.* New York: Holt, Rinehart and Winston, Inc., 1968.

DURR, WILLIAM K. *Reading Instruction: Dimensions and Issues.* Boston: Houghton Mifflin Company, 1967.

DURRELL, DONALD D. *Improving Reading Instruction.* New York: Harcourt Brace Jovanovich, Inc., 1956.

ELLINGSON, CARETH. *The Shadow Children.* Chicago: Topaz Books, 1967.

GILLINGHAM, ANNA, and STILLMAN, BESSIE W. *Remedial Training for Children with Specific Disability in Reading, Spelling, and Penmanship.* Cambridge, Mass.: Educators Publishing Service, Inc., 1960.

GOODMAN, KENNETH S. *The Psycholinguistic Nature of the Reading Process.* Detroit, Mich.: Wayne State University Press, 1968.

HAY, JULIE, AND WINGO, CHARLES E. *Reading with Phonics.* Philadelphia: J. B. Lippincott Co., 1960.

HEGGE, T. G., *et al. Remedial Reading Drill.* Ann Arbor, Mich.: George Wahr Publishing Co., 1955.

KOTTMEYER, WILLIAM. *Teacher's Guide for Remedial Reading.* Manchester, Mo.: Webster Division, McGraw-Hill, Inc., 1959.

LEFEVRE, CARL A. *Linguistics and the Teaching of Reading.* New York: McGraw-Hill, Inc., 1962.

MYKLEBUST, HELMER R. *Progress in Learning Disabilities, Volume I.* New York: Grune & Stratton, Inc. 1968.

Orton, June Lyday. *A Guide to Teaching Phonics.* Winston-Salem, N.C.: The Orton Reading Center, 1964.

Scott, Louise Binder, and Thompson, J. J. *Phonics: in Listening, in Speaking, in Reading, in Writing.* Manchester, Mo.: Webster Division, McGraw-Hill, Inc., 1962.

Shane, Harold G., *et al. Improving Language Arts Instruction in the Elementary School.* Columbus, Ohio: Charles E. Merrill Publishing Co., 1961.

Spache, George D. *Reading in Elementary School.* Boston: Allyn & Bacon, Inc., 1964.

Staats, Arthur W. *Learning, Language, and Cognition.* New York: Holt, Rinehart & Winston, Inc., 1968.

Umans, Shelley. *New Trends in Reading Instruction.* New York: Columbia University, Teachers College, Teachers College Press, 1963.

Veatch, Jeannette. *Individualizing Your Reading Program.* New York: G. P. Putnam's Sons, 1959.

Wilson, Robert M. *Diagnostic and Remedial Reading.* Columbus, Ohio: Charles E. Merrill Publishing Co., 1967.

INDEX TO GAMES AND ACTIVITIES